handmade books

A Step-by-Step Guide to Crafting Your Own Books

handmade books

A Step-by-Step Guide to Crafting Your Own Books

Kathy Blake

Photographs by Ted Morrison

A BULFINCH PRESS BOOK

Little, Brown and Company

Boston   New York   Toronto   London

First Edition

Designed by Barbara Koster

Library of Congress Cataloging-in-Publication Data

Blake, Kathy.
Handmade books : a step-by-step guide to crafting your own books /
Kathy Blake ; photographs by Ted Morrison. – 1st ed.
p. cm.
ISBN 0-8212-2220-1 (hc)
1. Bookbinding. 2. Books. I. Title.
z271.B6 1997
686.3 – dc21   96-51438

Bulfinch Press is an imprint and trademark
of Little, Brown and Company (Inc.)
Published simultaneously in Canada by
Little, Brown & Company (Canada) Limited

PRINTED IN SINGAPORE

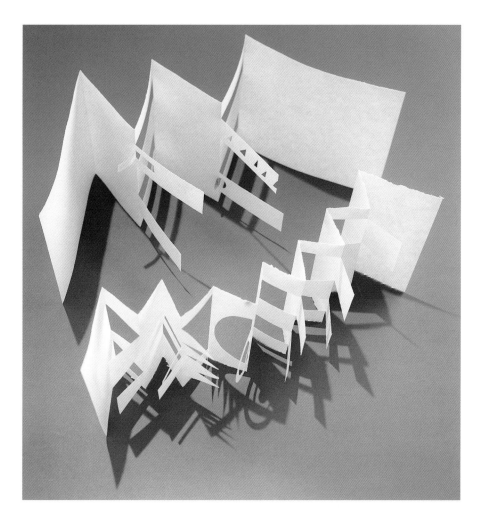

contents

Handmade Books:
Information and Inspiration

ecause we live in the information age, we're barraged with words and pictures on paper and on the air. Books, pamphlets, and magazines are sold and given away virtually everywhere we go — in supermarkets, doctors' offices, hotel lobbies, malls. We can plug into on-line communication or turn on a television for instant news from anywhere in the universe. Today, software manufacturers and publishers are developing CD-ROMs as a supplement to traditional books for information, entertainment, and interactive games.

Yet, there are those who love the look, the weight, the texture, the inspiration, and the mystery of books and, in spite of any new technology, will always love books. While millions of books are pumped out of machines every year, there are few crafts as rewarding as designing, planning, and creating handmade books.

Handmade Books takes you through the history of books, from the simplest rolls of paper to hardcover volumes, teaching you how to make your own beautiful books in various formats. You'll learn how easy it is to make personalized memo pads and how to quickly sew a folded signature to make a book to take along on a hike or to keep notes from a class. A book you've made yourself — whether you leave the pages blank or write poems or recipes in it for someone special — is a thoughtful, much appreciated gift.

The most effective way to learn from *Handmade Books* is to start making projects at the beginning of the book, because it is organized in a way that builds your knowledge and skill as you progress from chapter to chapter. By making an accordion book with hard covers, for example, you learn skills that can then be applied to making books with sewn signatures.

In *Handmade Books,* you won't find cookie-cutter instructions for making exact reproductions of the projects you see in the photographs. Instructions give you information, and photographs give you inspiration for ways you can take off from the basic to the imaginative.

As you walk through museums or shop, keep an eye out for books of various format and shape. Mark Twain said that our best ideas were stolen by the ancients, and that quip applies to books, too. Books made by artists and craftspeople centuries ago are some of the best we have and can spark our own creativity.

Many museums and university libraries have very old books that are sometimes on exhibit or available to see by appointment. Dr. John Lundquist at The New York Public Library generously allowed Ted Morrison to photograph a few of the treasures from the Oriental Division to illustrate this book, and curators there readily share their knowledge as well as their books with scholars, artists, and anyone interested in books.

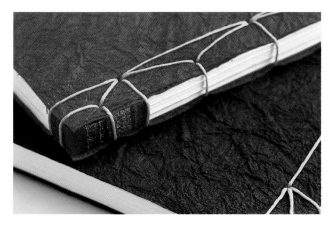

Thanks also to Kojiro Ikegami, author of *Japanese Bookbinding* (New York: Weatherhill, 1986). Her technique for making book cloth, as described in Chapter Two, is now widely used by bookbinders.

Special thanks to Katharine Lee Thuman and Manfred Koh.

I hope that you will use the ideas conveyed here to take off into your own flights of fancy and that you'll throw away preconceived ideas of what a book looks and acts like. Can a book be a single sheet of folded paper? Can a book's pages be cut in the shape of a mountain or a cat or a kimono? Is a plastic computer disk holder stuffed with loose pieces of paper a book? Yes.

Make some books and have some fun.

> ". . . of making many books there is
> no end . . ."
> Ecclesiastes 12:12

Chapter One

The History of Books

 or millions of years, history, genealogy, legends, lessons, and fables were stored only in human brains and passed on by the spoken word. Information necessary for survival — weather patterns, edible plants, the spirits that ruled the earth, water and sky, the habits of animals and fish, ways to build shelter and a fire, how to live in a group — as disseminated from one person to another and from one generation to the next in speech and song.

Beautiful primitive paintings and drawings of animals, hunting scenes, and even imprints of human hands survive on cave walls, although the meaning of much prehistoric art is now a mystery. These records may have been meant to convey information, to appease gods, or to record special occasions. Although they are records, they were certainly not a portable or convenient means of communication.

As the human race became more numerous, society became more complex. Living in towns and cities allowed people to specialize in an occupation. While some people farmed, growing the food to supply an entire village, others made bread or textiles or bricks. Bartering goods and services must have become complicated and too detailed for people to remember from season to season.

Early Accountants

The first known written records were accounts made by Sumerian tradesmen in ancient Mesopotamia (now Iraq) about 5,500 years ago. A square-tipped stylus was used to incise marks on clay tablets, which were then dried in the sun or in an oven. Around the same time, Egyptians had begun creating hieroglyphics and making records on stone and clay.

Writing — and, of course, reading — spread quickly throughout the ancient world. At last, permanent records could be kept and shared. Knowledge of astronomy, farming, religion, and history could be written on clay tablets. Laws were chiseled into stone stelae. Private messages could be sent long distances. In fact, important letters were sealed in tamperproof clay "envelopes," with the same message written on both the envelope and the tablet inside so that the recipient could be certain the message had not been altered between the time it left the writer and when it was delivered to its destination.

Sometimes people wrote messages on pieces of broken clay pots. There must have been many such pieces in villages where the pots were used for storing water, oil, and grain. Scribes wrote on the clay potsherds with brushes dipped in ink that was so permanent, it is still black and distinct today.

This edition of *The Declaration of the Rights of Man*, translated from French to Arabic in 1790 (the third year of the French Republic), is part of the massive collection of historical books in the Oriental Division of The New York Public Library.

Libraries of thousands of clay tablets stored in clay and stone holders were kept by the Mesopotamians. To keep track of the tablets during writing, drying, and storing, they were numbered, coded, and often titled. In effect, books as we know them were born five thousand years ago — long before paper was invented.

Many kinds of materials — including clay, stone, dried mud, silk and other fabrics, leather, leaves, tree bark, bamboo and other woods, metal, and ivory — can and have been used for writing. Parchment and vellum, which are both made from specially prepared animal skins, have proved to be very durable.

Examples of parchment scrolls and codices from more than two thousand years ago are still in good shape. But regardless of how hard tanners have tried to make flat sheets of parchment, it always tends to curl back to its original shape — the shape it had while on an animal.

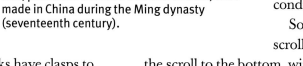

These accordion books with wood-block printed text, protected with silk-covered boards, were made in China during the Ming dynasty (seventeenth century).

That's why many very old books have clasps to hold them closed; a clasp prevents the parchment from curling. Parchment books were stored on bookcases upright, close together, to keep them flat, which is a practice we still use for book storage. Parchment was the most commonly used writing material until paper became available in the West during the Middle Ages.

From Papyrus to Paper

We get our word "paper" from *papyrus,* a rushlike stalky plant that grows in marshy areas along the Nile and other rivers. For centuries, Egyptians made sheets of material (also called papyrus) from these plants, using it for their own domestic needs and exporting much of it to Greece, Rome, and other cities. Very strong and lightweight, papyrus was in such demand that the plant was nearly extinct at times.

Writing on papyrus is best done with a brush, so scribes carried small pots of dry paint, a jar of water, and brushes that were originally made by chewing on the end of a stick until it was stringy. Papyrus records were rolled into scrolls and usually stored in clay jars, about ten to a jar. The Latins called the scrolls *volumen,* which became our word "volume." Many very old papyrus records still exist in remarkably good condition.

Sometimes writing on scrolls went from the top of the scroll to the bottom, with the writing running from edge to edge. Other times scribes wrote in columns about eight inches wide; the scroll was held by its two dowels, and each column was read in succession — as we read pages of a book.

While papyrus can be rolled easily, it doesn't fold well. Folded papyrus breaks quickly, making it good for scrolls or flat storage but not suitable for leaves of a book. Like paper, papyrus is fragile and easily destroyed. Natural disasters and, to a greater degree, war have destroyed millions of books of all types throughout the centuries. Fires — natural or not — volcanos, hurricanes, and floods have taken untold numbers of precious books. A library of more than 700,000 papyrus scrolls stored in a library at Alexandria was destroyed when Julius Caesar conquered Egypt. Even today, the destruction of books is recognized as a way of destroying a culture's past, present, and future.

About 1,900 years ago in China, paper was invented. The legend is that Ts'ai Lun beat ropes and fishing nets into a pulp, then poured it over a bamboo screen and let it dry. He pulled the finished paper off the screen and recognized its potential as a material for writing. Soon knowledge of the method spread through China, and other people experimented with using plant fibers, wood, and silk to make paper.

Tibetan "leaf books," handwritten on vellum, were made in the early twentieth century.

The secret of papermaking was confined to Asia for perhaps seven centuries. Then Muslim invaders took Chinese prisoners who divulged the secret of the process, soon Europeans learned of it, and paper mills were established wherever there was a good, steady water supply. It was only about two hundred years ago that machines for making paper were invented.

From Scrolls to Paperbacks

It took a long time to get from clay tablets to scrolls. And another long time from scrolls to the codices (bound, multisection books) that we're most familiar with. Meanwhile, probably to make storing and reading easier, someone folded a scroll into an accordion so that each column became, in effect, a page. These early accordion books — which are still made and used in the Far East — were held flat with boards on top and bottom. While not a radical change from scrolls, accordions are easier to read and take less space. Also, an accordion makes a good album because it can expand to accommodate added thickness.

By the fifth century, folded sheets of parchment were tied together with leather strips and were stored with wooden boards on top and bottom to keep them flat. Then someone used the loose ends of the leather strips to tie the boards to the book.

Eventually, the whole exterior of the book — boards and spine — were covered with leather. During the twelfth to fifteenth centuries, before binding machines or even printing presses had been invented, bookbinding, calligraphy, and illustration reached their zenith.

During the Middle Ages the production of magnificent books took a great deal of time, talent, work, and imagination. Wealthy patrons paid monks and scribes to create prayer books, Bibles, and songbooks with fabulously elaborate illustrations, often including portraits of the patron or the scribe in some of the drawings. Even today, the colors and gold leafing remain astonishingly bright and vivid in manuscript books from the thirteenth and fourteenth centuries.

It was at this stage of the history of books that the codex format we know came into common usage in the West. And during this time, more people were becoming literate and demanding books, which could be produced only in small quantities by hand. Again, inventors in China had the answer to the printing problem centuries before Europeans caught on. More than a thousand years ago, Chinese printers were carving whole pages of characters into wood blocks for printing books and scrolls.

Johannes Gutenberg, a fifteenth-century German goldsmith, invented movable type about 1438, revolutionizing printing and written communication forever. Movable type means that each letter is carved onto a single small block so that words, spaces between words, and lines of type can be restructured in many ways. While we credit Gutenberg with this invention, there is evidence that Koreans were using movable type in 1392.

For about four hundred years, pages were arranged by compositors who could assemble the letters into words and columns very quickly (even though they worked with letters that were backwards and upside down) and printed by pressmen who covered the plates with ink and

The Syriacæ Linguæ printed and bound in 1718 – a beautiful example of very early movable type.

Modern bookbinders find inspiration in the formats of ancient books.

pressed them onto paper with a screw-driven mechanism.

With mechanized printing, quantities of paper were needed to feed the presses, and the paper industry was born. From the tenth to the fifteenth centuries, European paper mills were filthy, unhealthy places to work. Ragpickers gathered cotton and linen, which were then soaked for weeks to break down the fibers, before workers beat the rags into tiny pieces so the resulting slurry could be formed into rolls of paper. By the mid-nineteenth century, papermaking had become more mechanized and less labor intensive.

Today, with the advent of computerized printing and illustration, few professional printers use the old-style metal type, but we continue to use some of the old terminology, such as "upper and lower case," which means that the capital letters were literally stored in the upper drawer and the small letters, in the lower drawer. Type size is still measured by the point-size system used by generations of typesetters.

Bookbinding also had to keep up with the speed of printing, and new, faster binding methods were invented. The format of codex-style books has changed little since the Middle Ages, but now with fully automated printers and binderies keeping production costs down, books and magazines are ubiquitous and readily available to almost everyone.

There are some softcover books that are printed on good paper, and even art books are sometimes bound with soft backs, but many paperbacks are self-destructive because they're printed on the very acidic wood pulp paper, which yellows and then disintegrates within a few years. About one-third of all books sold today are softcovers, or paper-backs, and while they don't last forever, they have gone far to make books cheap and easily attainable for many people.

There are those who predict that books will soon become obsolete, as computers become more fun, more accessible, and easier to carry around. But many of us who have picked up an old volume that had some long-dead owner's handwritten comments scribbled in the margins — or who have found ourselves circling passages in a novel or making notes next to a recipe — can't imagine a world without books.

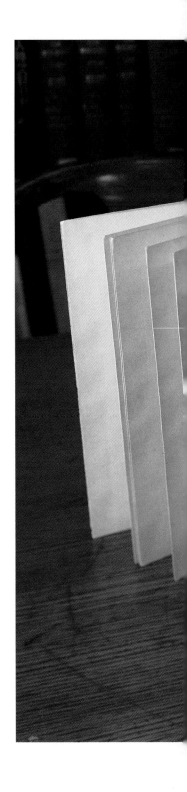

Printed in 1919, this Chinese accordion-style children's zodiac book was hand printed with wood blocks and still retains its fresh, lively colors.

Chapter Two

Paper and Equipment

ow your own bookmaking adventure begins. This chapter is a handy reference for information you need for any book you make. As with any craft, there are tools and techniques that you need for making books. Most of the tools required are household items; others are sold at art supply stores. But some tools and equipment are unique to bookbinding and are available only from well-stocked art supply stores or by mail order from bookbinding suppliers.

Naturally, paper is a very important element in bookmaking, and it is to your advantage to become familiar with various types, styles, sizes, and characteristics of paper.

Paper

Choosing Paper

Look at the paper around you right now. You'll see many shades of white — from sparkling to creamy — as well as colors, including "legal pad" yellow, robin's egg blue, "file folder" cream, and kraft brown. Feel the paper for its texture, stiffness, and weight. Some paper is pebbly and dry to the hand, while other paper has a glasslike slickness.

A paper's weight and stiffness helps determine its use in bookmaking. For example, the paper used to make file folders (known as card stock) is too stiff to be pages in a hardcover book but might be fine in some types of scrapbooks or photo albums. Thin, flexible typing paper, on the other hand, would be too lightweight to use in an album.

When making hardcover books, you'll also use bookboard (sometimes called binder's board, or millboard), which is pressed acid-free cardboard. Bookboard is available from bookbinding suppliers in various thicknesses; heavy bristol board is a good substitute.

Bookcloth is the very strong paper-lined fabric that is wrapped around the spine of hardcover books and portfolios. You can buy bookcloth by the yard or in smaller pieces from bookbinding suppliers. Or you can make your own by following the directions on page 24. Because it's made with paper as well as fabric, it shares some characteristics of paper.

In each chapter and project, there are recommendations for paper weight and stiffness for the various components of each book. Overall, you'll be off to a good start by learning a few traits that all papers have in common.

Equipment, tools, and paper ready for making books.

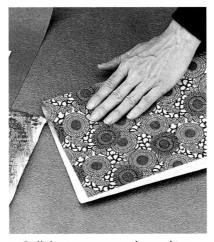

1 With just a little practice, you can feel a paper's grain. Roll a sheet of paper in half, lengthwise, and very gently tap the fold with the palm of your hand to get a sense of its resistance to light pressure.

2 Roll the paper crosswise and tap again. You will feel a difference in resistance to your gentle pressure. The grainline gives less resistance, whereas the crossgrain pushes back a little more. To remember which way the grain runs, make a light pencil line on the back of the paper, going with the grain. Find the grain of bookcloth in the same way.

3 Another way to check grain is to hold the paper against a very bright light. In many papers, you can see the direction in which the fibers run.

Grain

Tear a sheet of paper — newspaper will do. See and feel how the paper tears easily in one direction but resists and veers when you try to tear it the other way. The paper's *grain* is the reason it reacts like this.

Knowing which way the grain runs in paper, bookboard, and bookcloth is absolutely essential to successful bookmaking. Although paper is very thin, you'll be amazed at its strength and at how the grain insists on its own way. If you paste paper onto bookboard with their grains running other than parallel, the result will never lie flat, because the paper will pull the board out of shape.

To Find the Grain

Paper manufacturers often indicate the grain direction by underlining the dimension along which the grain runs. For example, a package of copy paper may read $8^{1}/_{2}$ x 11, indicating that the grain is parallel to the eleven-inch length of each sheet.

Checking a bookboard's grain is easiest when the board is large (bigger than 5 by 7 inches). Hold the board by opposite edges and gently pull them toward you until the board bends slightly in its center; then give the board a quarter turn and repeat. You will feel much more "give" when the board bends with the grain.

Grain is caused by the way paper fibers go

through papermaking machines. As wet paper pulp is poured onto a fast-moving belt that forms long rolls of paper, the tiny, hairlike fibers are pulled by the force of the machine until they're fairly parallel with one another. If wooden matchsticks were floating in still water and then hit a fast stream, imagine how the matchsticks would be forced by the water to run in the same direction.

Always, always find the grain of paper, bookboard, and bookcloth before cutting it. When planning a project, make sure all the grainlines run parallel to the spine of the book. This rule applies to all book projects, including scrolls, which roll and stay closed more easily if the grain runs parallel with the mounting stick(s), and accordion books, which fold and stay flat much more successfully when the folds are made with the grain rather than on the crossgrain.

Quality

You may feel overwhelmed with the wide choice of paper available to you. Take heart. While your choice of paper is a crucial element in the success of your book, your eye, hand, and common sense prevent you from making mistakes in your choices. You already know, for example, that the pages of an album need to be flexible and relatively heavy, so you wouldn't buy tracing paper for an album project.

Knowing how to judge the inherent qualities of paper is important because they affect the lifespan and durability of your books.

Briefly, paper is made by softening and beating fibers that when formed and dried are meshed together. Long, fine fibers make the strongest paper, so cotton, kudzu, bamboo, silk, and linen are ideal ingredients in paper. Wood pulp is much more commonly used and is less expensive, but the fibers

tend to be shorter. Wood pulp also has a high acid content.

Acidity   Acid-free paper may be made from neutralized wood pulp, rag (usually cotton or linen), or recycled paper. Whatever the paper's origin, the acid has been neutralized to a pH of 7.07 or higher. Acid in paper degrades the cellulose fibers, making the paper yellow and brittle. Newsprint and some construction and drawing papers are very acidic and disintegrate in a relatively short time.

You may want to use newsprint for making models of future projects, but using a high-acid paper for a time-consuming project is false economy. Many acid-free papers are labeled as such, but if there is no label, price can be an indicator. Relatively expensive papers, such as watercolor paper, handmade Japanese papers, and drawing paper are acid-free, although they often aren't so labeled.

Bond, cartridge, typing, or copier paper   Usually $8\frac{1}{2}$ by 11 inches or $8\frac{1}{2}$ by 14 inches, acid-free, recycled, and sold by the ream (500-page packages), this paper is used extensively in office printers and copiers and is available at all office supply stores, often in several pastel and neon colors. Check the grain of the paper before buying it for handmade book projects, just to make sure it runs the way you want it to.

Card stock or cover stock   This thin but stiff cardboard is often used for making file folders and postcards.

Decorative paper   Art supply stores carry decorated paper that is machine-printed or hand-colored or -marbled. Gift wrap is ideal for many book projects; comes in long, wide rolls; and costs less than art paper. Or decorate your own paper with markers, ink, block prints, paint, or crayons.

Handmade paper The textures and colors of handmade paper vary greatly — from small, fragile-looking brown sheets to large, white, heavy, smooth sheets of watercolor paper. In most cases, all four sides of handmade paper are deckled (a soft, fuzzy appearance), which can add a nice, feathery edge to the pages of a book or album. Most handmade paper is made in small shops in Asia, India, Italy, and North America. Wherever it originates, this paper is expensive, but often the textures and colors of the sheets make it worth its price for a special project.

Rag paper Artists use rag paper — papers with a high percentage of cotton, linen, or silk — for watercolor and etching. It is sold at art supply stores, usually in large sheets, which book artists can cut to meet their needs. You will also find rag paper, cut to standard office sizes, at stationers.

Recycled paper Some recycled paper is not bleached, so it carries specks of black type. Other paper is made using some recycled elements, including old clothing, thread, newspapers, cardboard boxes, or office wastepaper. Some is purely white or colored, making it indistinguishable from "virgin" paper.

Tracing paper, glassine, or onionskin paper Because these papers are thin and translucent, they can be used for decorative purposes in handmade books but are not strong enough for structural applications. (A sheet of these papers placed over a drawing or photograph gives the picture an attractive foggy look. Consider binding a sheet of glassine between each mounting page in an album to protect photos and add interest.)

Weight The most important thing a paper's weight tells you is how thick it is — it's also an indicator of price, with higher weights often costing more. In the United States, paper weight is measured in pounds per ream (500 sheets). Computer paper is usually 20- to 24-pound, and medium-weight drawing paper is labeled 60- to 80-pound. Heavy watercolor paper can weigh in at 300 pounds or more.

In other parts of the world, paper weights are much more precise. A square meter of the paper is measured and weighed, and the weight is indicated in grams. Copier paper, for example, weighs about 80 g/m^2, and drawing paper is about 150 g/m^2. In this system, paper heavier than 250 g/m^2 becomes card stock, and its thickness is measured in microns.

Bookboard

Originally, books were backed and supported with wooden boards, and the cardboard used to back "hardcover" books today is called bookboard. If you prefer a flexible book cover, as for some accordion books, you can use card stock or bristol board. If you're making large portfolios, consider substituting bookboard with thin particleboard or plywood, which makes a much stronger, stiffer cover.

Bookboard is sometimes called binder's board, Davey board, or millboard and comes in various thicknesses measured by a point system — the higher the number, the thicker the board. Heavy mat or museum board or acid-free rag boards can be used in the same way as bookboard but are more expensive.

For most projects 60-point or 80-point board is adequate, but for large-format or special-effect books, consider 100-point boards.

Be sure to check the grain and match the board's grain to the paper's before cutting.

Book makers choose from many colors and weights of paper for various applications.

Bookcloth

Bookcloth is fabric that is pasted to strong, lightweight paper, to prevent the fabric's stretching and to prevent glue from soaking through when the material is applied to bookboards. Bookcloth can be purchased by the yard in limited colors from bookbinding suppliers. But by making it yourself, you can choose among an almost infinite palette of colors and designs. You get the best results with tightly woven, natural fibers of cotton, linen, and raw silk in medium weight, such as the fabric used for making shirts.

Before you begin, be sure the grain of the paper and fabric match. Finding the grain of the fabric is easy, because the lengthwise grain of the fabric is parallel to the selvage, or woven edge.

**Materials you need
for making bookcloth:**

natural-fiber, closely woven fabric (such as cotton, linen, or raw silk), about 18 by 24 inches

smooth laminated tabletop or plywood

spray bottle filled with water

thin, strong backing paper, such as kozo or unglazed gift wrap, about 2 inches larger on each side than the fabric

a large sheet of scrap paper (not shown)

100% starch paste of mayonnaise consistency (see recipe on page 26)

paintbrush for paste

straightedge at least 18 inches long

wide, dry smoothing brush

rolled towel for tamping

To Make Bookcloth

1 Spread out the fabric face down on the work surface and spray the fabric thoroughly and evenly with water. Gently stretch the fabric and smooth out any wrinkles.

2 Place the backing paper on a large sheet of scrap paper. Apply paste liberally and evenly with a brush, starting all strokes from the center of the paper and pulling the paste to just beyond the edges.

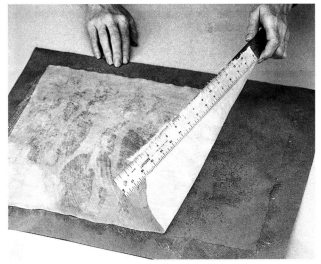

3 Put the flat side of the straightedge down on one of the short sides of the paper and slowly pull the straightedge up; the wet, pasted backing paper will come up with it.

4 Make sure the grain of the fabric and the grain of the paper are running in the same direction, then carefully place the backing paper over the damp fabric so there is a two-inch margin of paper on all four sides.

5 With a wide, *dry* brush, smooth out the wrinkles and air bubbles, brushing from the center out to the edges.

6 Tamp lightly all over the backing paper with a rolled towel to help the fibers of the paper and fabric mesh together.

7 To make sure the bookcloth dries flat and smooth, you'll temporarily affix it to the work surface. Apply a thick layer of paste all around the edges of the backing paper. Lay a tab of paper on one edge of the backing paper (to make a "handle" for separating the bookcloth from the table after it dries).

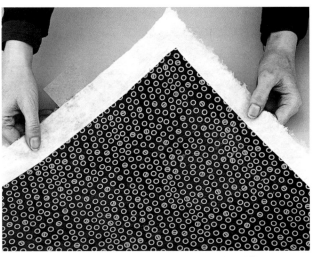

8 Put the wet bookcloth on the smooth, clean work surface to dry. Again, using the straightedge to pick up the paper and fabric together, turn the whole thing over so the fabric side is facing up. Brush additional paste around the edges again to make sure they stay put as the bookcloth dries.

9 Drying time will be at least four hours, depending on the climate. When the bookcloth is completely dry, insert a knife blade under the tab to loosen, and then gently pull the bookcloth off the work surface.

10 If the bookcloth feels strong and slightly stiff, it is ready to use.

Adhesives

Some glues create an irreversible bond, meaning that whatever adheres together cannot be separated again after the glue dries. Other adhesives – those that are "archival" – are water- or chemical-soluble, and therefore reversible. You'll use various adhesives when you cover bookboard with paper, make bookcloth, and affix a scroll to rods, among many other processes involved in making books. Each project in this book specifies the best adhesive for the job. While it may seem easier to have one all-purpose glue on hand, different applications require different adhesives. Using the right adhesive is vital to making a beautiful, long-lasting book. The primary book-making adhesives are listed below.

PVA, or polyvinyl acetate This fast-drying white glue dries clear and stays flexible but is not reversible.

Starch paste Cornstarch or rice flour, when mixed with water and cooked, makes a smooth, shiny paste that is strong but water soluble, and therefore reversible. Starch paste is very easy to make:

¼ cup cornstarch or rice flour
¼ cup cold water
2 cups boiling water

In a bowl, stir the cornstarch or rice flour with cold water until the mixture is smooth and thick. Gradually stir in boiling water, mixing well until the mixture is thick and glossy and begins to look transparent. (It will continue to thicken as it cools and can be thinned with water. If there are lumps in the paste, push it through a fine sieve with a wooden spoon.) Let the paste cool before using. It can be stored covered in the refrigerator for up to two days.

Methylcellulose or wallpaper paste Dry mixes are available in hardware stores; look for brands with methylcellulose as the only ingredient, with no toxic pesticides. These pastes are reversible when dry and can be used instead of starch paste, but they are not as strong.

Mixture Some applications, such as adhering bookcloth or paper to bookboards, require a make-it-yourself 50/50 mixture of PVA and methylcellulose or starch paste because the methylcellulose or starch paste will slow the drying time, allowing you to reposition and perfect the fit.

Rubber cement The only time you use rubber cement is when making memo pads; otherwise, it is never used in bookmaking.

Spray mount Glue-in-a-spray-can is useful for some jobs, such as dry mounting. Be sure to follow the directions on the can.

Tools

You can make gorgeous books with very little special equipment. In fact, you probably already have some of the tools you need. It's a good idea to have a tackle box or toolbox to keep your book-making tools together, so you have them handy and clean when you need them. With the following equipment, you can make every project in this book:

Bone folder This pointed, wedge-shaped tool is necessary for scoring, folding, and creasing paper. Bone folders are available in various sizes from bookbinding suppliers and catalogs.

Craft knife A knife with a replaceable blade (such as a #11 X-Acto) or a rotary cutter (such as quilters and other textile artists often use) is necessary for cutting paper and lightweight board; for cutting heavy boards, a carpet knife or box cutter is optional.

Paper scissors Scissors with very long blades, or any scissors that can stand up to the rigors of cutting paper, are indispensable.

Table paper cutter A table paper cutter can cut boards and stacks of paper on the square and is an option for those who cut a lot of paper.

Cutting mat "Self-healing" mats protect work surfaces and come in many sizes. The mat should be hard rather than spongy. They are available at fabric and art supply stores.

Straightedge A metal straightedge — not plastic — is ideal for guiding long cuts with a craft knife.

T-square It should be metal and at least 12 inches long, or a metal triangle with right angles.

Awl Sometimes called a "potter's tool" by bookbinders, a wood-handled awl makes holes for binding. You could also secure a heavy darning needle in the end of a short, thick dowel for making holes in paper.

Drill Another tool for making holes in paper, a hand-cranked or electric drill goes through a thick stack of paper or boards but tends to grind rather than make a smooth hole.

Hole punch An office-style hole punch can be used for making decorative effects.

Darning needles Long, thick needles with big eyes are sold at fabric stores, most discount stores, and many grocery stores.

Thread Avoid polyester or cotton-covered polyester for book projects because it stretches — linen, cotton, or silk thread is a bit more expensive but is stronger and does not stretch. Professional bookbinders and conservators insist on linen, which comes in various sizes from bookbinding supply shops and catalogs.

Brushes Paint brushes of various widths, both artists' and hardware style, are used for decorating paper and applying adhesives.

Tools for cutting paper and bookboard include a table paper cutter, saw, drill, craft knife, scissors, razor blades, safety blade cutter, and rotary cutter.

Chapter Three

Scrolls

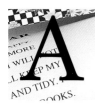

As a way of making and keeping records, scrolls are the simplest book form and are almost as old as writing. About 4,500 years ago, Egyptians began making papyrus scrolls by beating the stalks of papyrus plants and then pressing them together in two layers at right angles to each other. The sheets were brushed with a gummed sizing agent to prevent the fibers from absorbing ink; then the sheets were pounded to force the fibers to interweave. After drying in the sun, the papyrus was coated with another solution to keep it pliable.

This method allowed scrolls up to forty feet long and usually about twelve inches high, although they were sometimes cut down to three or six inches high for easier handling. After sticks were attached to the ends of the long sheets, they were rolled, labeled on the outside, and stored in jars.

The oldest known papyrus record is the Prisse Papyrus, which was made and written around 2500 B.C. and is now in the Louvre in Paris. It contains the philosophy of "an aged sage"

Facsimiles of a twelfth-century Japanese ten-volume edition of the Buddhist iconography.

who wrote his views about living a wise and moral life. Samples of ancient papyrus records are in the collections of most major museums.

Some of humankind's most important and beautiful concepts — such as the Egyptian Book of the Dead, Buddhist sutras, and the Jewish Torah — have been recorded on scrolls. While the scroll is not a common book format today, we can exploit its form for making our own records and artwork.

A scroll is a natural container for recording seasonal activities, such as the development of a garden, a year in a child's life, or a family vacation. A special scroll can be used as a guest book. World history or one's own life story in the form of a time line with stories and illustrations may become a precious heirloom. An unfurled scroll on a table or on the floor can be used by more than one person, so children especially enjoy the opportunity to paint, draw, or write together on a scroll. A group might write a letter or birthday greetings on a small scroll to send to a faraway friend.

When choosing paper for a scroll, first consider its use. If your scroll will be a keepsake or if you plan to spend many hours

The words on this scroll were written and printed on a computer before the pages were glued together. The text rolls into a paper-covered tube.

drawing, making calligraphy, or writing poems on it, choose sheets of good quality paper. You will probably have to paste them together to form a long strip. Check the grain of the paper before you paste. The paper's grain should run parallel to the dowels so that it rolls easily with the grain rather than against it. Glue carefully, making sure that the strip is straight and that the pages are even, top and bottom, by frequently holding a straightedge against the edges and making adjustments before the paste dries.

If, on the other hand, your scroll will be used for a class of kindergarten children to make drawings of spring flowers or dinosaurs, you can use less-expensive paper that is sold rolled, such as kraft paper, gift wrap, shelf liner, or butcher paper.

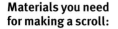

**Materials you need
for making a scroll:**

two dowels of any
thickness

dowel caps, such as
wooden knobs, metal
or wooden curtain
rod finials, or buttons
(optional)

white glue (optional)

paint for dowels and
caps (optional)

a long roll of paper

straightedge

pencil

scissors or craft knife

ribbon or cord long
enough to wrap at
least twice around
the scroll, plus a few
inches

PVA glue

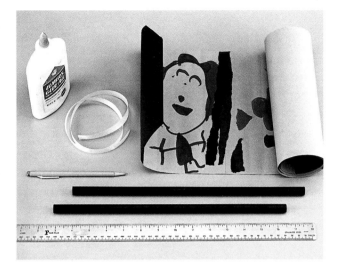

1 If you are using wooden dowel caps and want to paint them the same color as the dowels, attach the caps to the dowels before painting. (You may have to whittle the ends of the dowels with a sharp knife before attaching the dowel caps with white glue.) If you are using buttons or metal fittings as dowel caps, paint the wood dowels before attaching the caps with white glue.

2 On both ends of the paper, draw a pencil line about one inch from the edge to use as a guide for lining up the dowels. (If your dowels are very thick, draw a line further in from the end of the scroll so the paper will cover the dowel's entire circumference.) Cut triangles off all four corners to make rolling the paper around the dowels smoother.

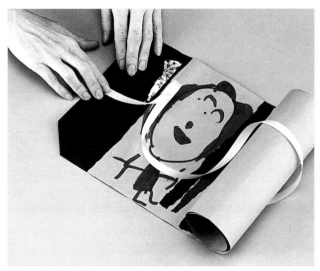

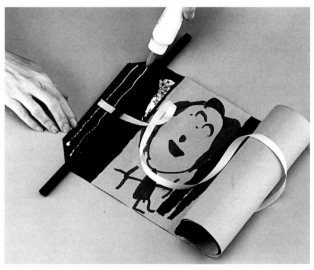

3 The ribbon is attached to only one end: place the length of ribbon or cord in the center of one edge of the paper — one end of the ribbon should be flush with the edge of the paper — and affix it with a spot of PVA glue, and then tie a knot in the ribbon's free end to prevent it from raveling.

4 Make two or three rows of glue on the paper, using the pencil line as a guide.

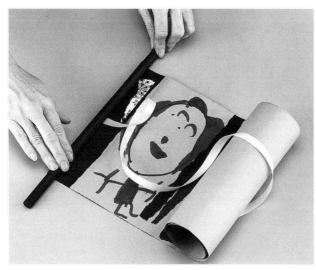

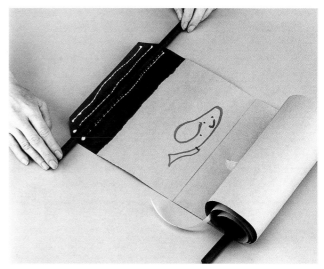

5 Roll the dowel and paper together and smooth the paper down so the dowel is secured.

6 Repeat the process, but without the ribbon, on the other end of the scroll.

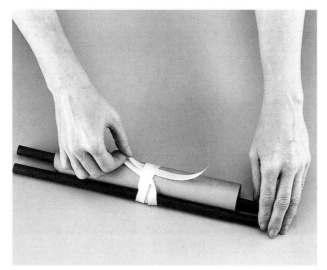

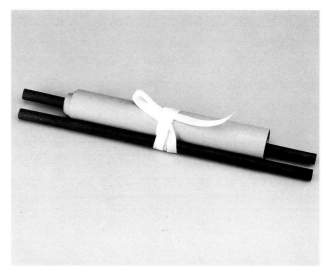

7 When the glue has dried, roll the scroll onto the dowel that does not have the ribbon attached; then wrap the ribbon around the scroll and secure it by tucking the end of the ribbon under itself. You may apply a strip of paper to the outside of one end of the scroll and write a title on it.

8 The finished scroll can be stored in a vase, or you can make a paper envelope or fabric pouch for it. (The scroll shown here was designed by Emma Morrison.)

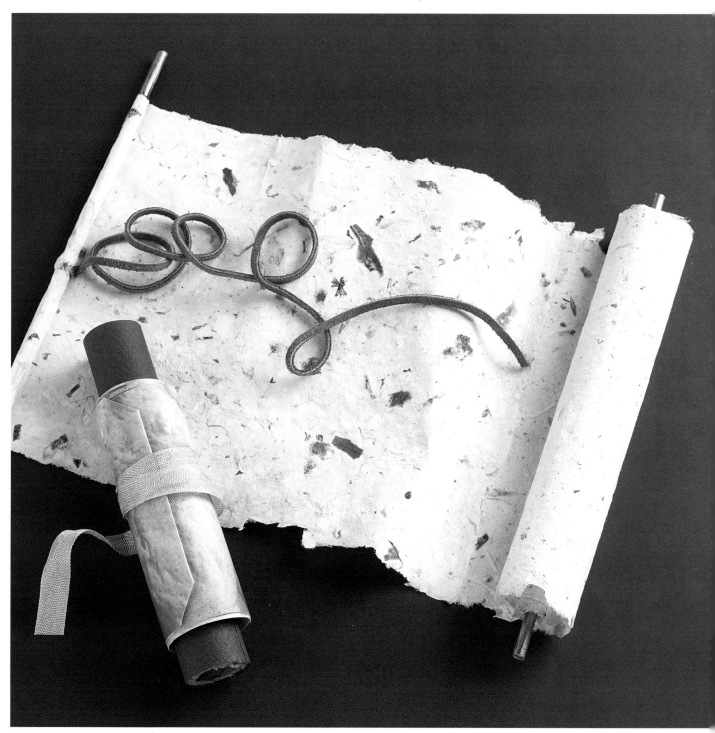

These scrolls made with handmade paper were inspired by ancient Japanese scrolls.

Chapter Four

Accordion Books

After people had made scrolls for centuries, someone realized that if the scroll's long strip of paper were folded accordion-style, it would be easier to store and use. At its most basic, an accordion book is made of a continuous strip of folded paper.

Ancient Romans, however, made their own style of accordion books long before there was paper. They wrote on wax plates that were made by carving out a shallow, flat hollow on one side of a sheet of wood, which was then filled with black wax. They wrote on the wax with a bone, wood, brass, or bronze stylus. A little heat would easily erase marks on the wax. Sometimes thin leather strips would be used to tie together two of the wax-filled boards (with the waxed sides facing each other). When more than two boards were tied together, they were attached to one another accordion-style for carrying and storing.

Another type of accordion-style book is still used in India and Southeast Asia, where palm leaves are readily available. Palm leaves are prepared for writing by cutting them to uniform size, boiling them in milk or water, and then drying and rubbing them smooth. To hold the leaves together as a book, two holes are drilled through each leaf before the leaves are written on; then a string is inserted through all the leaves. The string is tied loosely enough so that the leaves can be pulled apart for reading.

Because palm leaves are fragile and quickly destroyed by humidity and insects, important documents and scriptures were often written on metal or ivory plates the same size and shape as palm-leaf books.

In Tibet, temple libraries are filled with books of a similar size and shape to palm-leaf books, but these

Some pages in a bound book can be accordion-folded, as in this 1828 edition of *Precis du Systeme Hieroglyphique des Anciens Egyptiens ou Recherches* by Champollion – the first translation of Egyptian hieroglyphics.

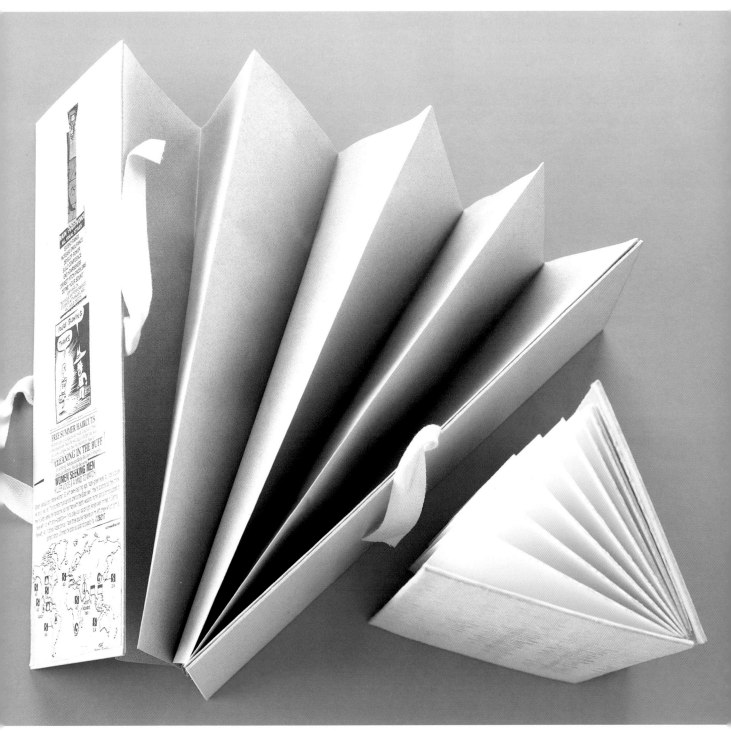

Hardback accordion books can include ties or remain loose.

holy texts are loose-leaf. A cover and bottom made of wood or heavy cardboard hold together hundreds of very thin, strong sheets of paper, and the books are read by turning each leaf over, with care taken to keep the leaves in the correct order. Sometimes the loose stack of sheets is lightly wrapped in a silk scarf.

The invention of accordion books as we know them had to wait for writing material other than papyrus, because papyrus is too brittle for repeated folding.

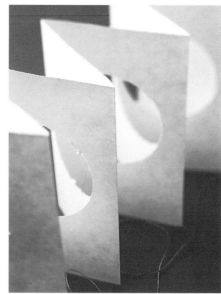

Parchment and vellum were used in scrolls and may have been used in early accordion books as well. Parchment was first used around 500 B.C. but didn't become widely used until several centuries later. Parchment is made from the skin of a sheep or goat but is tanned in a different manner than regular leather is. Vellum is made in a similar way from the skin of a calf. The nature of parchment and vellum causes them to roll rather than lie flat, so when they are used in an accordion, the covers need to be heavy enough (for example, made of wood) to secure the materials, or ties can be attached to the four sides of the cover to keep it closed.

An accordion book can be stored flat or upright on a bookcase. It can also stand on a table, either pulled open or with two

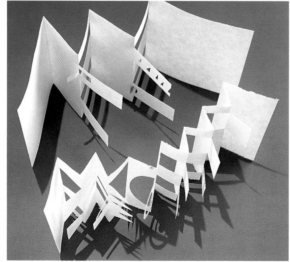

adjacent edges of the cover close together so that the pages stand out. Accordion books are ideal scrapbooks or albums because they expand to accommodate any thickness of material you add. Side-bound books tend to bulge at the open side when filled with drawings or photographs.

The "flag book," a variation on the accordion, was invented by Hedi Kyle, book artist and conservator in Philadelphia. Kyle makes basic flag books by first making an accordion book with very narrow pages — only about an inch wide. Then she pastes two or more pieces of paper or card stock to each of the narrow accordions. When you paste the pieces of paper on alternating sides of the accordion folds, the papers point in opposite directions when you pull the covers apart. Store and display a collection of baseball cards or postcards by making them the "pages" in a flag book. Or mount photos on pages made of heavy stock paper. Otherwise, flag books are simply fun to play with and design. (See photograph on page 47.)

Accordion books are sensually pleasing to the eye, hand, and ear. You can play with an accordion book by pulling the covers apart and moving them around to see how the pages flutter, creating a rustling sound.

Cut and pull out shapes from the edges of an accordion book to make "flags."

Make your accordion books with very strong, thin paper, such as goshu, or lightweight bristol board, poster board, construction paper, kraft paper, shelf liner, or copier paper, depending on the particular use you have in mind.

You'll find many uses for the accordion-style book. A small one with a few pages made of construction paper and no covers could be a greeting card. A larger accordion made with bristol or poster board is a terrific album for mounting, storing, and displaying photographs, drawings, or postcards. Take an accordion book to the beach or on a vacation to make sketches or record your impressions and memories.

Materials you need for making an accordion book:

paper
craft knife
straightedge
disposable work
     surface
scrap paper
brush
100% starch paste
bone folder
ruler
heavy weights
ribbon or cord
     (optional)

To Make an Accordion Book

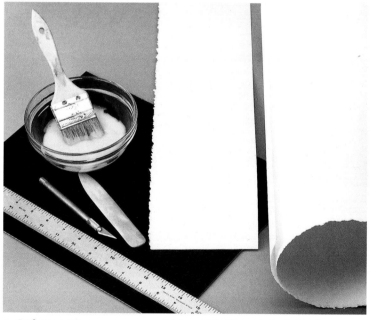

1 Before cutting your paper with a craft knife and straightedge, check its grain, as described on page 20. The grain must run parallel with the way you will fold the paper. If you're using a long, continuous roll of paper, skip to step 4.

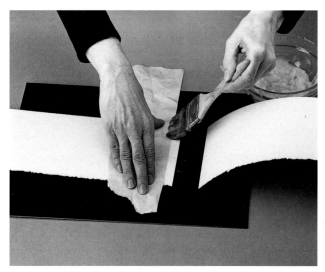

2 Create a long length of paper by pasting pieces of paper together: working on a disposable surface, first with scrap paper mask all but about ½ inch of one edge of a sheet of paper. Brush paste on the edge of the paper.

3 Place another piece of paper overlapping the pasted edge by ½ inch, then rub the edge with your fingers or bone folder until it adheres. Continue adding lengths of paper until it's as long as you like.

4 Whether you have a long, continuous roll or whether you have pasted sheets together, determine how wide you want the pages of the book. Measure with a ruler, then with the bone folder make indent marks in the paper where the folds will be.

5 Turn the ruler and score the paper with the bone folder at the mark.

6 Lift the paper and rub the bone folder along the score mark to fold it.

7 Turn the paper to its other side and repeat the process so you have a fold that turns in the other direction.

8 Protect the folds by covering them with scrap paper, then rub each crease well with the bone folder.

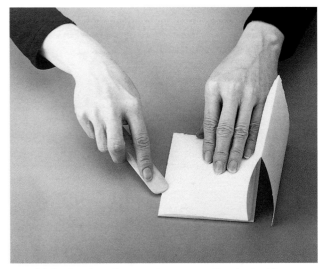

9 Fold the book and press the creases firmly. At this point, you can let the accordion rest under heavy weights for 24 hours to flatten.

10 The accordion is made — ready for covers to be added or for use as it is.

If you opt to let the front of the accordion serve as the book's cover, you can attach a cord to tie it closed. Cut a piece of cord long enough to wrap around the book at least once, then glue the cord to the front or back of the book. Or make a slit in one of the covers of the book, insert the cord, and then tie a knot in it or glue it securely to the inside of the cover. Wrap the cord around the book, then secure it loosely by slipping the end of the cord under the loop.

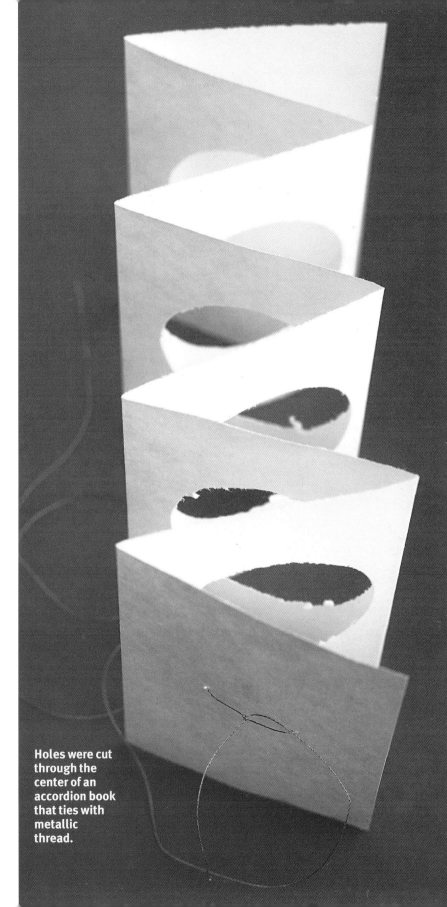

Holes were cut through the center of an accordion book that ties with metallic thread.

To Add Hard Covers to an Accordion Book

Materials you need for adding hard covers to an accordion book:

bookboard

pencil

ruler

craft knife (or small scissors)

scrap paper

decorative cover paper that is strong but flexible

mixture of 50/50 PVA/starch paste adhesive

glue brush

bone folder

ribbon or cotton twill tape (optional)

plastic wrap or Mylar®

weight

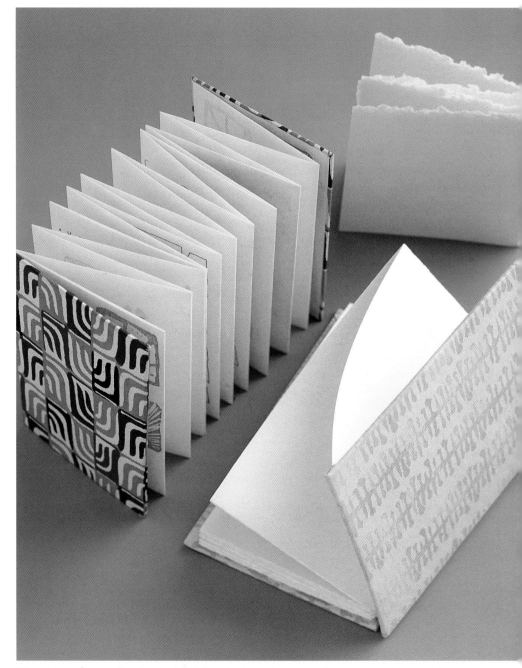

The pages of accordion books hold drawings or photos easily, because this book format expands naturally.

1 Check the grain of the bookboard and make a pencil line on it to mark the lengthwise grain. The grainlines of the book's paper, the bookboards, and cover paper must all run the same way. Measure and cut two pieces of bookboard the same size as, or no more than ⅛ inch larger on each side than, the folded book.

2 Find the grain of the cover paper. Measure and cut two pieces of cover paper so that each projects ¾ inch beyond the edges of all four sides of the bookboard.

3 Apply the cover paper: place the cover paper face down on a sheet of scrap paper. Brush a thin coat of 50/50 PVA/starch paste mixture, beginning every stroke in the center and pulling the brush just beyond the edge of the cover paper. Discard the scrap paper.

4 Carefully place the bookboard on the pasted paper, being careful that there is an even ¾-inch margin around all four edges.

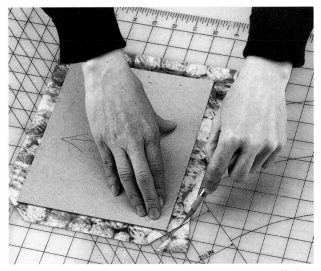

5 With a craft knife or small scissors, cut triangles off all four corners, leaving a margin of paper at each corner equal to twice the thickness of the bookboard, which allows you to cover the board's corners securely with paper.

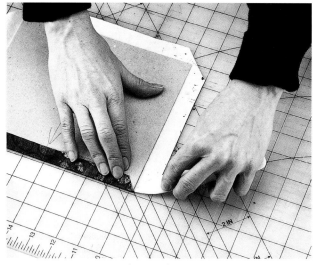
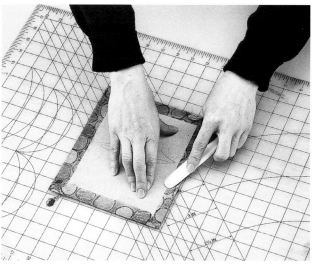

6 Starting at the head (the top) of the cover, with the flat side of the bone folder raise the paper up and over the bookboard and rub it down well. (If the paste has dried on the edges of the paper, carefully apply more with a brush.) Use the point of the bone folder to rub down the tiny edge of the paper you will see extending at the corners, which helps cover the corner smoothly.

Now raise and fold the tail side (the bottom) of the paper over the bookboard and rub it well.

Raise and fold over the fore edge (opposite the spine side), then the spine side.

Repeat with the other cover paper and bookboard.

7 Roll the flat of the bone folder gently over the corners to flatten any points that have formed. Then rub the outside of the cover with your fingers or the flat side of the bone folder to smooth out any air bubbles.

8 If you like, you can add ties at this point, before attaching the cover, as shown in the example in the photograph on page 37. Measure two lengths of ribbon or cotton twill tape equal to the width of the bookboard plus enough to tie easily at both sides. Lightly glue the ribbons at the exact center of the uncovered sides of the boards. The ribbons will lie across the centers and will extend beyond the edges of the boards. The ribbons will be further secured when the boards are attached to the book.

9 Attach the book to the covers: place a piece of scrap paper between the first and second pages of the accordion book to protect the book from paste, then with a brush carefully apply mixture of 50/50 PVA/starch paste to the first page of the accordion book. Discard the scrap paper.

Carefully place the first page of the book onto the uncovered side of the bookboard; adjust so there is an even margin at each edge of the bookboard. Rub it with your fingers or the flat side of a bone folder to smooth out any air bubbles. In this way, the first page has become the "lining" for the front cover.

Repeat this procedure with the back page of the book and the other bookboard. To be sure the book dries flat, put plastic wrap or Mylar® between the covers and the first and last pages so the pages don't absorb excess moisture from the damp covers. Wrap the book in several layers of scrap paper. Weight the folded, closed book until the covers are completely dry, about 8 hours or overnight.

ash wednesday

i
n
f
e
b
r
u
a
r
y
s

This accordion flag
book was made by
glueing rectangles
of paper onto the one-
inch-wide "pages"
of the book. When the
book is opened, the
pages flutter and move.

Chapter Five

Bound Single Sheets

Until the Industrial Revolution, all paper was made by hand, and size and thickness could vary greatly from one manufacturer to another, or from one day to another. Today, machine-made paper is consistent in weight (thickness) and is cut to standard sizes, although the standards vary slightly in different parts of the world.

While the standard sizes of today's paper may be predictable, the range of colors, textures, designs, and weights available is stunning. Browsing through a paper catalog or walking through a paper supplier's showroom can be awesome and inspiring. You'll find recycled papers sprinkled with tiny specks of black; neon colors; colorful confettilike squares embedded in white; stately watermarks in pale, creamy 100 percent cotton paper; and paper printed with borders or watercolorlike images.

Then take a look at artists' papers, including watercolor paper in rough or hot-pressed textures and various weights;

In 1736, *The Mustard Seed Garden Manual* was hand painted on silk-like paper; then the pages were sewn together in traditional Japanese style.

pastel or charcoal paper with deep or shallow "tooth" in a rainbow of colors; and the wonderful textures and colors of natural handmade papers imported from Asia and India or created at small mills in the United States.

All these papers, in every size and color and in many weights, have potential as text blocks or covers for handmade "bound single sheet" books. Newsprint can be used for making models or prototypes, but the paper will yellow and crumble within a few years, so don't invest your precious time and creativity in a project made with newsprint.

Start making single-sheet books by experimenting with typing or computer paper. With a stack of the most common paper, you can make a book in minutes. With or without including a cover, you can hold a stack of paper together with staples or Chicago screws. Or by placing the paper on a piece of cardboard and painting one edge of the stack with rubber cement, you have a memo pad in little more than an instant.

In this chapter, you will learn

Japanese
binding
decoratively
binds single
pages and,
at top,
folded
signatures.

how to make books with Japanese binding, starting on page 56. At first glance, the sewn design looks very complicated, but you'll be surprised at how simple it is once you start. Because of the way books bound Japanese-style open, strong lightweight paper such as washi or rice paper is best. You can make them with ordinary copier paper, although it is a little more brittle than long-fibered washi.

The cover material for these softcover books needs to be light and flexible, too. For the best results and long life, look for momigami (crinkled paper), marbled paper, or kozo paper. The most important feature of the thread or ribbon you use (besides its decorative effect) is that it not stretch. To test thread you're considering, hold a 6-inch length and pull it gently. You'll be able to feel stretching in polyester and other synthetics, but not in linen, cotton, or silk.

One creative bookmaker used a Japanese-bound book as an unusual sort of journal. He pasted his horoscope predictions from the newspaper into the book each day and made notes about which of the cautions and encouragements were accurate. Another handmade book, small and narrow enough to fit easily in a shirt pocket, served as an expense account record.

During a class reunion or at a wedding reception, you might pass out sheets of paper and markers for guests to draw and write on, then collect the papers and make a book as a keepsake. At the end of a school year, a summer project might be sorting and binding children's artwork into books. Write your thoughts or poems or favorite quotations in a small book to keep or give. Or make a book with a few large pages and let your children draw and write in it as a gift for grandma.

The Parts of a Book

Now you will begin making codices, which are books in the style we are most accustomed to — with leaves that are bound on one side. Get acquainted with the bookbinders' standard names for the parts of a book:

spine: the edge of the book where the text is attached

fore edge: the side of the book opposite the spine

head: the top of the book

tail: the bottom of the book, opposite the head

height: the measurement from the head to the tail

width: the measurement from the spine to the fore edge

text or text block: the pages or leaves of the book

Here, books were sewn with two strands of pearl cotton thread, in black and yellow, and orange plastic "thread."

To Make Memo Pads

Materials you need for making your own memo pads:

a stack of paper

one piece of cardboard cut the same size as the paper

clamps or clothespins

rubber cement

To make the most of recycling paper, you can use the blank side of wastepaper from the computer or copier for making memo pads, or cut up unused paper if you prefer. Use any color bond paper and cut it to the size you like.

1 Tamp the stack of paper and the cardboard together, making sure that the side to be glued is flush and even.

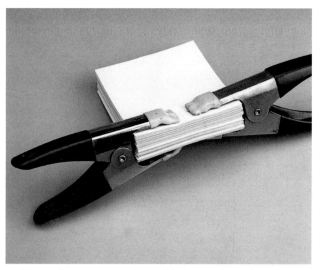

2 Clamp the stack together, with the cardboard on the bottom, applying clamps on opposite sides, leaving free the side that will be glued.

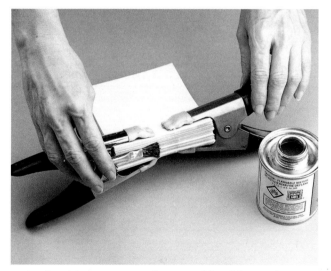

3 Apply rubber cement to the even side of the stack, rubbing the ends of the brush into the edges of the paper, including the cardboard, to be sure every sheet is glued. Let it dry at least two hours, then apply more glue and let it dry overnight.

4 Remove the clamps.

Materials you need for making single-sheet softcover books:

text paper (such as typing, notebook, copier, or kraft)

cover material (flexible paper of the same weight or heavier than the text paper, such as cover stock; file folder material; gift wrap; drawing, pastel, or charcoal paper)

paper cutter, craft knife, or rotary cutter

clamps or clothespins

pencil

ruler or spring divider

awl, hole punch, hand drill, or other device for making holes (if using Chicago screws, brass fasteners, or ring binders)

choice of binding material:
staples and stapler
grommets and grommet tool
Chicago screws
brass fasteners
ring binders
report holder

string or ribbon (optional)

darning needle (optional)

Single pages held together with ring binders and clips.

When deciding on the size of your book, before cutting your paper and cover material, remember to add a margin at the top or side for making holes or stapling. Usually 1 inch is enough space. The grain of the paper and cover must run parallel to the side that is being bound.

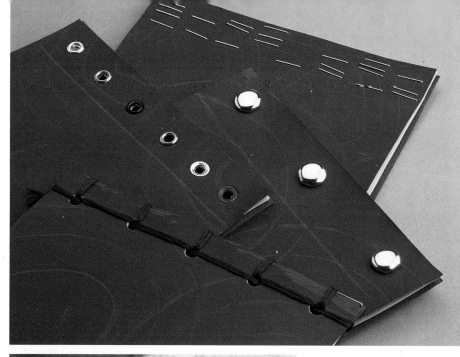

1. The type of binding you choose determines how thick your book can be. For example, if you're binding with a desk stapler, you'll find that the stapler will go through only a limited thickness of paper. The same is true of a grommet tool or the Chicago screws or brass fasteners you use. So, you may want to experiment before beginning to bind your book.

2. Cut the pages and cover material to size with a paper cutter, which can take several sheets at a time, or measuring carefully, cut each sheet with a craft knife or rotary cutter. Be sure the grain of the paper runs parallel to the spine of the book (the side where the book is bound).

   Sandwich the text block between the two covers. Tamp them on your work surface to make sure they're aligned, then stabilize the stack with clamps or clothespins on two sides.

3. If you're stapling or using grommets to bind the stack, do so now in any arrangement you choose at the top or side, making sure to use enough staples or grommets to secure the stack. (If you like, you can thread string or ribbon into a darning needle, then run it through the grommets to add color and strength.)

4. To bind with Chicago screws, brass fasteners, report holders, or ring binders, you need to make holes in the top or side of the stack, at least 1 inch from the edge. Measure and mark, using a ruler or spring divider, where each hole will be made; then with an awl, hole punch, or drill, make holes straight through the entire stack — front cover, text block, and back cover.

5. Now apply or insert the fastener of your choice to hold the book together. Remove the clamps.

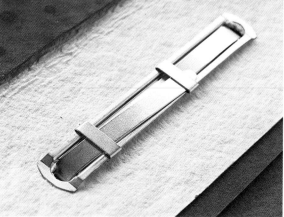

The pages of these books are held with a report holder (left), ribbon, grommets, brass fasteners, and staples.

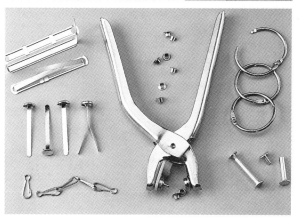

Sample of binders for single sheets (clockwise from top left: report holders, grommets and tool, ring binders, Chicago screws, clips, and brass fasteners).

To Make Japanese-Bound Softcover Books

**Materials you need
for making a Japanese-
bound book:**

stack of lightweight, strong
    paper

two sheets of strong, flexible
    cover material

clamps or clothespins

a strip of scrap paper to use
    as a guide for making
    holes: cut it 2 inches wide
    and as long as the height
    of the book; mark it with a
    pencil line down the
    middle, then fold it
    crosswise into 6 sections

strong sewing thread
    (100% cotton, linen,
    or silk, or 6- strand
    embroidery floss) or cord,
    string, or hemp fiber

darning needle

awl

board to protect the table
    (optional)

Choose Japanese — or washi — papers for this
book format because the papers are lightweight
and flexible, yet very strong. Japanese-bound books
are fun to make — once you get the rhythm of the
sewing. While the process seems difficult when you
read about it, when you do it yourself, you'll find that
it goes along in a very logical way. And you'll be very
pleased with the results. Be sure to read and follow the
sewing directions carefully the first time you make a
Japanese-bound book; then you'll find you can
eventually do it without following so closely. In
addition to these step-by-step photos, on page 58 you'll
find an illustration to use as a quick reference for the
sewing pattern.

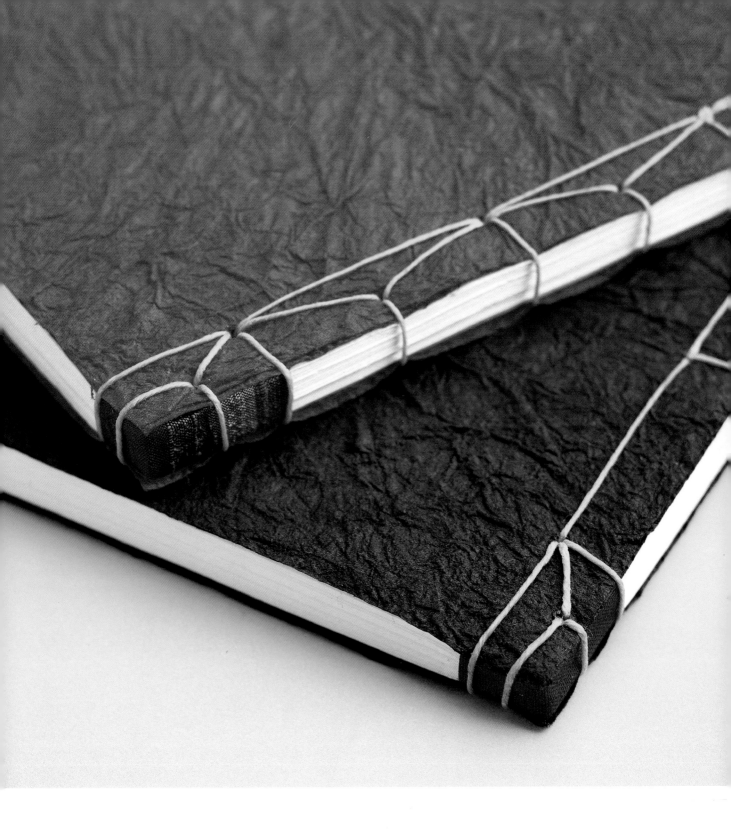

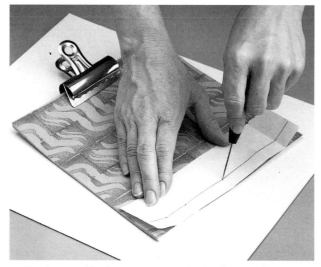

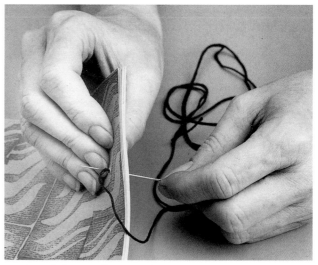

1 For the text block, you can use single sheets of paper (as shown here) or try the traditional Japanese method of folding sheets in half and placing the *folded edges at the fore edge of the book* (the loose edges of the sheets will be toward the spine).

2 Sandwich the text block between the covers and tamp the covers and paper together to even, then clamp at the fore edge. Line up the guide sheet with the spine of the book and push the awl through the entire stack at the fold lines on the guide sheet. Discard the guide paper.

3 Thread the needle with a length of thread that is six times the height of the book. Begin sewing in the second hole from the bottom by pushing the needle through from the *back* to the *front* (1). Leave a 4-inch tail of thread, and take the needle around the edge of the spine and then back up through the same hole, again from the *back* to the *front* of the book (2).

Refer to the diagram below for stitch numbers.

Japanese Binding Stitch

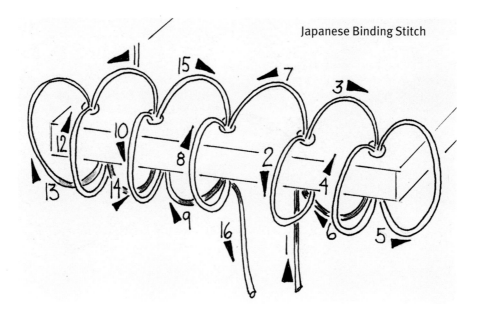

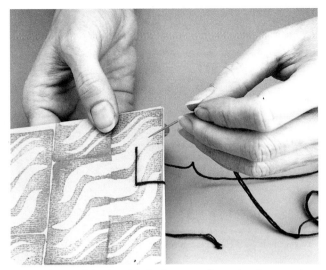

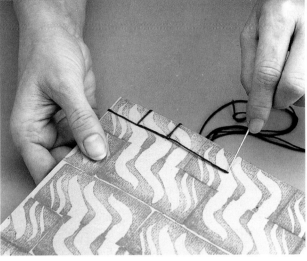

4   The front of the book is facing you; from the *front* to the *back* of the book, push the needle through the first hole from the bottom (3). (This creates a stitch parallel to the spine.) Take the thread around the edge of the spine and then, again from *front* to *back,* push the needle down through the same hole (4).

5   Now make the corner stitch: the front of the book is facing you, and the thread is at the back of the book; take the thread around the edge of the bottom (the tail) of the book and then push the needle through the first hole, down from the *front* to the *back* of the book (5).

The thread is at the back of the book; take the thread up from *back* to *front* up through the second hole (parallel to the spine) (6).

The thread is at the front of the book; take the thread from *front* to *back* through the third hole (parallel to the spine) (7), then around the edge of the spine and back through the same hole again, *front* to *back* (8).

6   Take the thread from *back* to *front* through the fourth hole (parallel to the spine) (9), around the edge and then up, *back* to *front,* through the same hole (10).

The thread is at the front of the book; take the thread from *front* to *back* through the fifth hole (parallel to the spine) (11), around the edge of the spine and then from *front* to *back* through the same hole (12).

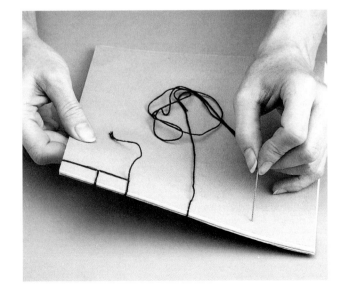

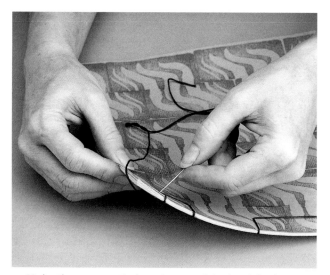

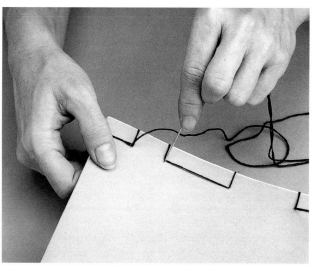

7 Make the corner stitch at the top of the book in the same way you made the bottom: take the thread around the top edge (the head) of the book, then down from *front* to *back* through the fifth hole (13).

8 Push the needle through the fourth hole, *back* to *front* (14).

Take the thread parallel to the spine and push the needle into the third hole, *front* to *back* (15).

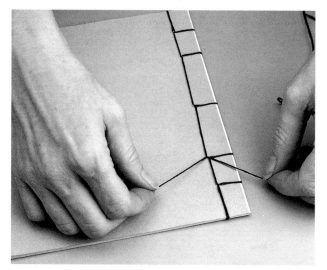

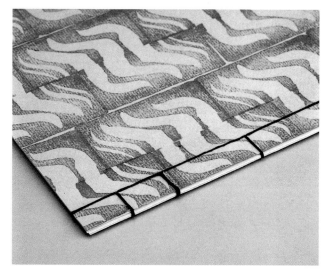

9 To tie off, remove the needle from the thread, take the long end of the thread to the second hole (where you began), and make a square knot directly over the hole. Snip off the ends of thread. If you like, you can add a dot of glue to the knot to secure it, and with the awl, snuggle the knot into the hole to hide it.

10 The stitching on the completed Japanese-bound book will look the same, front and back. If you have more than five holes, follow the same pattern, but make more stitches.

The finished Japanese-bound book was made with yellow pastel paper hand printed with a carved eraser and red ink.

Chapter Six

Single-Signature Books with Soft or Hard Covers

aking a single-signature book brings the satisfaction of making a "real" book because it looks and behaves like the book format we're most familiar with. A signature is a stack of paper that has been folded with the grain and then sewn or stapled together. Many magazines and pamphlets are single-signature, softcover books. The single-signature book is also called a pamphlet binding.

The term "signature" originated because binders made marks on each book section as a guide to keeping them in the proper order for gathering and binding the printed book. Today, in binderies where books and magazines are put together, a signature is a large sheet of paper that is machine-folded into sixteen or thirty-two pages, then trimmed.

When making single-signature books, you can make a soft cover using paper that is slightly heavier than the text paper and simply folded around the

Pull the cover off a notebook, then make a new cover with your choice of paper – and make a sleeve for it, if you like.

text and sewn in at the same time that the stack is sewn together, or you can make a hard cover with bookcloth at the spine and paper covering the bookboard.

Now that you have made and played with accordion books, you can see the evolution from accordions to single-signatures. We can imagine someone, most likely a Roman law clerk in the fourth century or so, folding and sewing a stack of parchment sheets into the first codex, the technical name for a book made of folded bound sheets. In those days, stacks of four sheets of parchment were stacked and sewn in the center, making a signature of eight leaves, which were then sent to a scribe who copied the text before a set of signatures was bound together and covered with thin wood boards. Everything was then held with metal clasps. The strong boards and clasps were needed to prevent the parchment from curling.

You may want to write or draw on the pages before you bind the book, or you can make a blank

Softcover single-signature books can have many looks.

book that can then be used for writing poems or as a diary or sketchbook. Many book artists use computers and/or color copiers to design their books' pages before binding, which you can do, too. Or with paint or colored pencils, you can make borders and pictures or write on the pages before or after binding.

A softcover book can become an elaborate birthday, graduation, or congratulations card for a friend. Make a long, narrow hard-bound book with its spine on a short side and employ it as a guest book. And imagine what a wonderful keepsake you would have by making pencil sketches and written notes of a vacation or family reunion in a book you've made yourself.

If you have a pamphlet-style booklet, such as a program from a play or opera or a catalog from an art show, you can give it a new soft or hard cover by following the instructions in this chapter. Or if you buy a lined notebook that is made of folded sheets, you can remove its cover and add a new one, as shown at far right in the photograph on the next page.

When you are choosing text paper to make a brand-new book, consider its grainline first — can the paper be folded with the grain and still be wide enough? Then feel its weight. You can use thick paper for a single-signature book, but you will then have few pages because by using many sheets of thick paper, the finished book will be ill proportioned and unwieldy, and the fold will refuse to lie flat.

Bond, computer paper, office stationery, graph paper, and lightweight drawing paper are all good choices for text in single-signature books.

For the cover of a softcover book, use heavier but flexible paper, such as watercolor, card stock, construction paper, heavyweight drawing paper, or light but strong decorated Japanese paper. Or you can trim an existing file folder to size and use its fold as the spine of your softcover book.

When planning hardcover books, you have the fun of choosing coordinating text paper, cover material, bookcloth, and endpapers. Cover paper can be cut from gift wrap, decorated Japanese paper, pastel paper, lightweight watercolor paper, kraft paper, or construction paper.

Traditionally, endpapers are marbled, but you can use any plain or decorated text-weight paper that promotes the spirit of your book. Children's finger paintings or abstract crayon drawings are often good choices for covers and endpapers. Bookcloth that you have made or bought can cover a narrow or wide area or the entire cover of the book — there are no rules about the width of the bookcloth, but whatever pleases you is good.

Enjoy choosing the colors and textures for making your single-signature books with soft or hard covers.

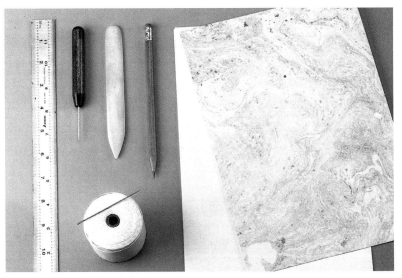

Materials you need for making a softcover single-signature book:

craft knife or paper cutter

text paper: computer paper, bond, notebook paper, or strong, lightweight Japanese paper (or make the text from an existing pamphlet)

decorative cover paper that is strong but flexible

bone folder

ruler or spring divider

pencil

awl

darning needle

strong thread (linen, silk, or cotton)

1 If you are covering an existing pamphlet or playbill, remove and discard the staples or thread from the centerfold.

   If using new paper, determine the finished size of your book and use a craft knife or paper cutter to cut the text paper and the cover paper to the height and twice the width of the finished size. For example, if the finished size will be 7 inches high by 5 inches wide, cut the paper 7 by 10 inches. The number of pages in your signature is limited by the thickness of the paper because a signature that is too thick will be bulky and unwieldy. Be sure the grain of the paper and the cover paper run parallel to the spine of the book.

2 Neatly fold the cover paper and each sheet of text paper in half and press the folds down with the bone folder. Place the text block inside the cover.

3 Prepare to sew the signature and cover together: with the stack open and flat with the centerfold toward you, measure and mark with a ruler or spring divider the middle of the fold, then make two more marks, each at least 1 inch from the head and tail. With an awl, pierce three holes at the marks.

   Turn to page 69 and see steps 5 to 10 for directions on how to sew a signature. You will sew the book together through the cover and text block — ignore references to the hinge used in the hardcover version. When you finish sewing, you will have a completed softcover book.

While the pages of a single-signature book can be bound with staples in the spine fold, here the pages are sewn with linen thread.

To Make a Hardcover Single-Signature Book

Materials you need for making a hardcover single-signature book:

craft knife or paper cutter

text paper: computer paper, bond, notebook paper, or strong, lightweight Japanese paper (or cover an existing pamphlet)

endpaper to match or contrast with cover paper (marbled paper, quality gift wrap, or decorated bond paper)

bone folder

kraft paper or bookcloth for hinge

ruler or spring divider

pencil

awl

darning needle

strong thread (linen, silk, or cotton)

bookboard

scrap paper

mixture of 50/50 PVA/starch paste adhesive

glue brush

weight

bookcloth to match or contrast with cover paper

decorative cover paper that is strong but flexible

100% starch paste

plastic wrap or Mylar®

Note: The endpaper is cut the same size as the text paper; the boards, bookcloth, and cover paper are cut to size after the signature is sewn.

1 As when making a softcover single-signature book:

If you are covering an existing pamphlet or playbill, remove and discard staples or thread from the centerfold.

If using new paper, determine the finished size of your book. With a craft knife or paper cutter, cut the text paper, endpapers, and the cover paper to the height and twice the width of the finished size.

Be sure the grainlines of the paper and the cover run parallel to the spine of the book.

Fold each sheet of text paper and fold the endpaper in half, *decorated sides facing each other.*

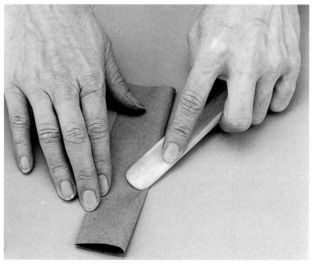

2 Lay the endpaper on the worktable, *decorated side up.* Place the text block on the endpaper. Fold the entire block in half and run the bone folder along the fold to crease.

3 Cut a piece of kraft paper or bookcloth the same height as the text block and 3 to 4 inches wide. (This becomes the hinge.) Fold it in half lengthwise and crease it with the bone folder; then place its fold on the outside of the text block's fold.

4 Open the signature and make three pencil marks in the centerfold for holes — one at the middle and the others at least 1 inch from the head and tail.

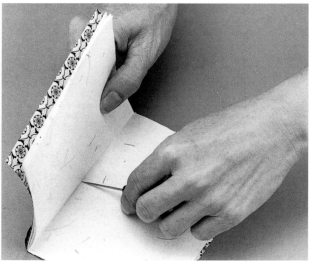

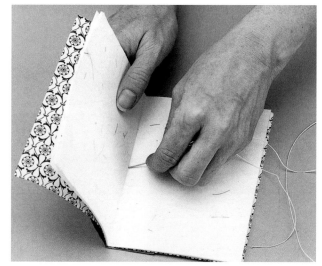

5 Push the awl through the marks, from the inside to the outside of the spine, piercing the text block, endpaper, and hinge.

6 Thread the needle with thread that is three times the height of the book, and begin sewing a figure eight by pushing the needle through the middle hole from the *inside* to the *outside* of the spine through the entire stack — the text, endpaper, and hinge — and leave a 4-inch tail of thread.

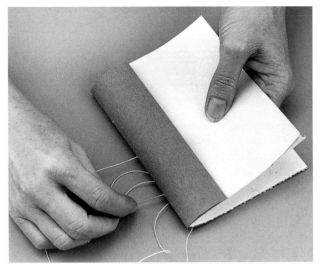

7 From the *outside*, push the needle through the bottom hole to the *inside*.

8 Push the needle from the *inside* to the *outside* through the top hole (skipping the center hole).

9 Now, from the *outside*, push the needle through the center hole to the *inside*. There will be a long strand of thread running from the top hole to the bottom hole with the two thread ends coming out of the center hole.

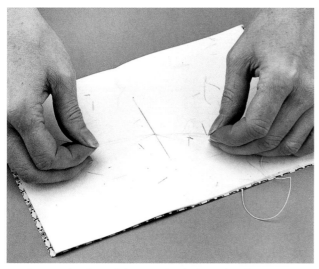

10 Secure the thread: be sure both thread ends are underneath the long strand so that when you tie the knot, the long strand is caught and secured by the knot. Tie a square knot; snip the ends to about $\frac{1}{2}$ inch.

11 Close the sewn signature and draw a line on the hinge $\frac{1}{4}$ inch from the spine; repeat on the other side of the book.

12 Cut the bookboard: measure and cut the boards $\frac{1}{8}$ inch larger than the text block around the head, tail, and fore edge. The spine edge of the board butts up against the line marked on the hinge ($\frac{1}{4}$ inch from the spine).

13 Draw a line on the bookboards approximately $1\frac{1}{2}$ inches from the spine side as a placement guide for the bookcloth.

14 Put a sheet of scrap paper under the hinge to protect the text from the adhesive. Brush one side of the hinge with mixture of 50/50 PVA/starch paste.

15 Apply the bookboard to the hinge: pull out the scrap paper and mount a board on the pasted side of the hinge, with one edge of the board along the line marked on the hinge. Make any necessary adjustments to be sure the board extends evenly on all sides. (There should be a $\frac{1}{8}$-inch margin between the board and text block on the head, tail, and fore edge sides.)

In the same way, apply the other board to the other side of the book, then let the book sit under a weight until dry — at least 4 hours.

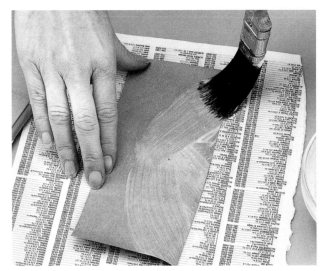

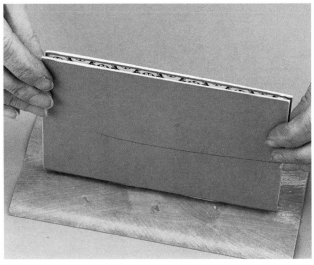

16 Measure then cut a piece of bookcloth to cover the spine: in height the bookcloth should measure $3/4$ inch beyond both the top and bottom of the boards, and it should be wide enough to extend to the lines you drew on the boards (approximately $1\frac{1}{2}$ inches from the spine side). Draw a line down the center of the "wrong" side of the bookcloth.

17 Brush the "wrong" side of the bookcloth with the 50/50 mixture adhesive.

18 Hold the book closed and place the spine of the book on the line drawn in the center of the bookcloth, with $3/4$ inch extending beyond both the head and tail.

19 Put the flat side of the bone folder under one side of the bookcloth and raise the bookcloth up and rub it onto the board with the broad side of the bone folder.

20 Lay the book down and turn it on its other side, then rub that side of the bookcloth to be sure it adheres to the boards. (If it doesn't stick, the paste has dried, so apply more mixture to the bookcloth.)

 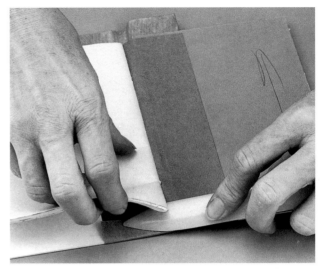

21 With the long edge of the bone folder, rub the bookcloth into the crevice that forms between the board and the spine of the text (the sewn signature will be extending beyond the boards about ¼ inch). Keep rubbing until you're sure the bookcloth is adhered to the spine. Repeat on the other side.

22 Open the cover of the book and grasp the closed text block at the head of the book; pull the spine-side corner of the closed text block (just above the first sewing hole) gently toward you so that the edge of the text block is separated from the hinge.

With the cover still open and the text block still held closed, use the bone folder to pull the ³⁄₄-inch bookcloth extension up and over the hinge. (If the adhesive has dried, reapply the 50/50 mixture to the extensions.) With the point of the bone folder, vigorously rub the extensions into the groove between the boards until the extensions are smoothly adhered to the hinge.

Repeat this procedure on the tail of the book.

23 Measure and cut the cover paper so it extends ³⁄₄ inch beyond head, tail, and fore edge of the boards. On the spine side, measure and cut the cover paper so that it just barely covers the edge of the bookcloth by about ¹⁄₈ inch.

24 Apply the cover paper: place the cover paper face down on a sheet of scrap paper. Brush a thin coat of 50/50 PVA/starch paste mixture, beginning every stroke in the center and pulling the brush just beyond the edge of the cover paper.

25 Carefully place the pasted paper just over the edge of the bookcloth, making sure that the edges extend evenly (3/4 inch) at the head, tail, and fore edge.

26 With a craft knife or small scissors, cut triangles off the corners at the head and tail ends of the fore edge side, leaving a margin of paper at each corner equal to twice the thickness of the bookboard, which allows you to cover the board's corners securely with paper.

27 With the flat side of the bone folder, raise the fore edge of the paper up and over the bookboard and rub it well on the top and edge. Use the point of the bone folder to rub down the tiny edge of the paper extending at each corner, which helps cover the corner smoothly.

28 Raise and fold the head side of the paper over the bookboard and rub it well on the top and edge.

29 Raise and fold over the tail side.

30 Roll the flat of the bone folder gently over the corners to flatten any points that have formed. Then rub the outside of the book with your fingers or the flat side of the bone folder to smooth out any air bubbles.

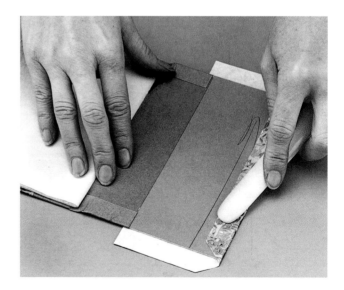

The small book on top is nearly completely covered with printed bookcloth; the middle book would be an ideal guest book; and the bottom book in traditional proportions and colors was designed to be a journal.

31 Apply the endpapers to the cover: open the cover and place scrap paper between the endpaper and the first page of text. Brush 100% starch paste onto the "wrong" (undecorated) side of the endpaper. As always, begin each stroke at the center of the paper and pull the brush out to just beyond the edges. Remove the scrap paper.

32 Slowly and carefully bring the cover up and over the pasted endpaper; rub the closed cover with your hand to smooth the endpaper, but do not open the book. Repeat the procedure with the other cover.

33 Without opening the book, slip plastic wrap or Mylar® between the cover and the text so the damp of the cover doesn't filter into the text block. (The reason you shouldn't open the cover is that doing so would pull the endpaper out of alignment.) Place several layers of scrap paper beneath and on top of the book to absorb extra moisture. Place a weight on the book, changing the scrap paper as it gets damp. Depending on climate, drying time is at least 8 hours. Your book will then be smooth, flat, and beautiful.

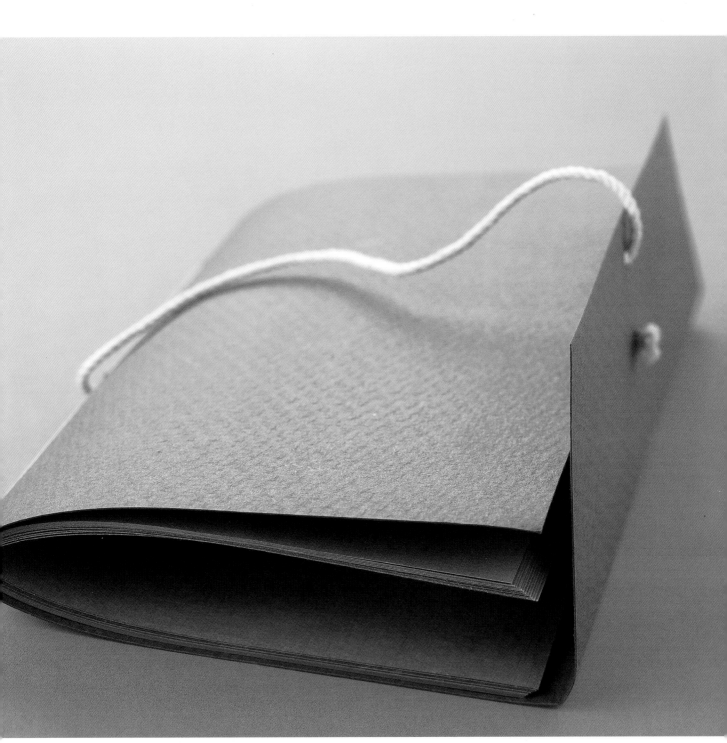

The fore edge of one side of a softcover extends around the text. Light rope was threaded through the flap and wraps around the book. This little book is pocket-size for traveling.

Chapter Seven

Albums and Portfolios

aking care of special family photographs often means placing them in albums for safekeeping. And once photos are safely in an album, they can be viewed repeatedly without getting damaged. If you make your own albums, they can be of any dimensions you like, the pages can be of a color that will enhance your pictures or drawings, and you can create personalized covers.

Heavy watercolor paper was hand painted for a softcover album.

You can easily achieve a special effect in an album by inserting sheets of glassine or onionskin paper between each album page. The frosty, translucent paper will soften the appearance of the photographs before you turn the page, and the additional paper also protects the pictures from friction.

After a special event, such as a graduation, baby shower, family reunion, birthday party, or wedding, you can make an album and mount photos that were taken at the event. Or to commemorate a

milestone wedding anniversary, have old photographs copied and place them in an album you've made.

Albums can also be used as scrapbooks for keeping certificates, newspaper clippings, or letters. The paper that newspapers are printed on is very acidic, which is the reason it yellows and gets brittle after a relatively short time. So to be sure that the clippings you want to save will survive, make color or black-and-white copies of them and store the copies in your scrapbooks.

By the way, storing letters in albums or scrapbooks can be a wonderful way to keep a family diary. One family of eight adult siblings is close-knit but far-flung. So to keep in touch, they have a quarterly family newsletter. For the newsletter, each sibling writes an update about what's happening in his or her family's lives and sends it to the person designated as the newsletter editor. That person compiles the "articles," prints them out on a computer, and then mails them to the extended family. Throughout the

A small portfolio ties at three sides to hold photographs securely inside.

years the newsletters are kept in albums that can be taken out and enjoyed anytime.

A word of warning about purchased photo albums: the inexpensive albums widely sold these days that have "magnetic" pages will slowly but surely destroy photographs and other paper because of the chemicals in the mounting boards. Rather than risk losing irreplaceable pictures, be sure the paper in your albums is acid neutral.

Making an album is very similar to making a book of bound single sheets but differs slightly in that adequate space is needed between each page at the spine side to accommodate the thickness of the items you will add. Without that "ease" of extra space built in, the album would bulge at the unbound side. For hardcover albums, cover the bookboards with bookcloth rather than paper because there will be much stress on the hinge of the covers and paper will eventually tear.

Sturdy portfolios are nice to have around for storing and carrying loose papers of various sizes. Make portfolios for holding stationery, stamp collections, wallpaper samples, pressed flowers, or postcards or for carrying drawings, sheet music, or photos.

You will find that making a portfolio is similar to making a single-signature hardcover book, except that you don't sew in text — a difference that makes the process quicker and easier. In fact, you might make a list of all the people you will give gifts to in the next few months and set up production, assembly-line-style, for making several portfolios at once. Cut all the bookboard, bookcloth, papers, and ties; then assemble them. Cover each portfolio with different papers so that each gift is individualized.

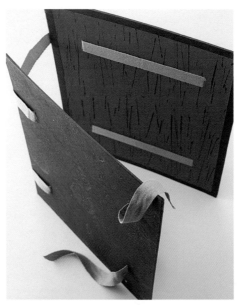

Cotton twill was threaded through slits made in covered and lined boards. This portfolio format allows an almost unlimited amount of paper to be stored within.

Portfolio spines can
be covered with
bookcloth or left open.

To Make a Softcover Album

**Materials you need
for making a softcover album:**

paper cutter, craft knife, or
rotary cutter

text paper (watercolor paper,
heavy rag stationery, or
pastel paper)

cover material (flexible paper
of the same weight or
heavier than the text paper,
such as file folder material
or pastel or charcoal paper)

ruler or spring divider

straightedge

bone folder

scrap paper

clamps or clothespins

pencil

awl, hole punch, hand drill, or
other device for making
holes

sliding report holders or brass
fasteners

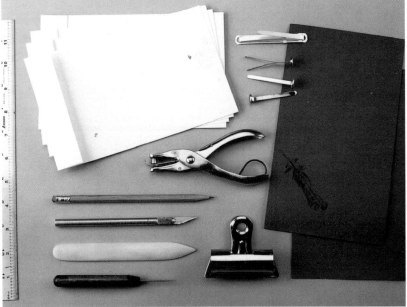

1 Before you cut the cover paper and the text paper, be sure to
allow at least 1 inch on the spine side to be folded over as
"spacers" between the pages. For example, if your album will
be 11 by 14 inches, with the spine on an 11-inch side, cut the
text and cover paper 12 by 14 inches. After the folds are made,
the finished size will be 11 by 14 inches.

The grain of the text paper and cover material must run parallel
to the spine.

Cut the pages and cover material to size with a paper cutter,
which can take several sheets at a time or, measuring carefully,
cut each sheet with a craft knife or rotary cutter.

Brass fasteners hold this softcover album together, allowing easy addition or removal of pages.

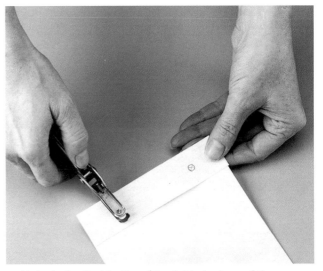

2 One sheet at a time, measure 1 inch or more of the paper and cover material at the side that will be the spine of the album. Use a straightedge and bone folder to score the paper where it will be folded, then fold it on the score line and rub down well with the flat side of the bone folder.

3 Make holes for binding. (The folded edges of the covers will be arranged so that they hide the clasps that hold the album together. When making the holes, do not unfold the text paper — make the holes *through* the folded pages. But for the covers, unfold them and make holes only on the narrow fold margins.)

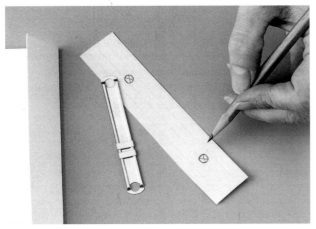

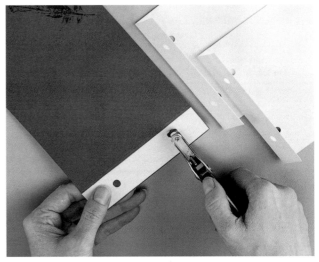

4 If you are using brass fasteners, with a ruler or spring divider and pencil, measure and mark two places for holes on both covers and the text paper.

   If you choose to use a sliding report holder, measure and mark the distance between the uprights of the holder on a piece of scrap paper cut the same size as the folded margin. Use the marks on the scrap paper to make holes with an awl, hand drill, or hole punch.

Note: A very large album needs more than two brass fasteners or more than one sliding report holder. Use your judgment as to how much support your album needs to be sturdy.

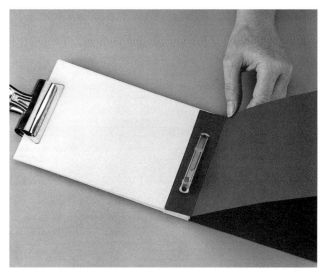

5 Put the covers aside. Hold the text pages together and tap them on the spine side to be sure they're aligned and flush; clamp them together, leaving the spine side free.

Turn both covers so *the folded edges face the inside of the album,* then sandwich the text block between the covers.

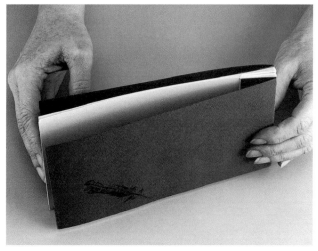

6 With the text pages still clamped together, open the covers and insert the brass fasteners or the sliding report holders through the holes made in the covers and text. Remove the clamps.

A softcover album can protect snapshots, a baseball card collection, or postcards.

To Make a Hardcover Album

Materials you need for making a hardcover album:

ruler

bookboard

paper cutter, craft knife, or rotary cutter

¼-inch acrylic spacer, or a spacer cut from bookboard exactly ¼ inch wide and at least 6 inches long

bookcloth

scrap paper

mixture of 50/50 PVA/starch paste adhesive

glue brush

scissors or craft knife

bone folder

decorative paper (to line covers)

weight

text paper (watercolor paper, heavy rag stationery, or pastel paper)

clamps or clothespins

awl

linen thread

darning needle

1 The grain of the bookboard, text paper, bookcloth, and lining paper must run parallel to the spine.

Determine the finished size of your hardcover album, then make the covers: measure and cut two pieces of bookboard for the covers. Cut two more pieces of bookboard the same height as the cover pieces and 1 ½ inches wide — these will be the hinge pieces that fold under the covers and hide the binding.

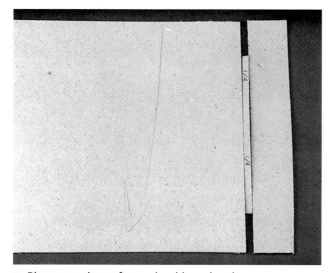

2 Place one piece of cover bookboard and one narrow hinge piece side by side; place the ¼-inch spacer between them with their edges touching, then measure the entire area of the two bookboard pieces plus the spacer, all measured as one piece. (The ¼-inch space between these pieces will allow the hinge to be folded back after the bookcloth is applied.)

3 Cut two pieces of bookcloth, each measuring ¾ inch larger on each side than the total measurement for the two pieces of bookboard, including the ¼-inch space.

4 Place a piece of bookcloth face down on a sheet of scrap paper and brush on mixture of 50/50 PVA/starch paste, beginning every stroke at the center and pulling out just beyond the edges of the bookcloth. Discard the scrap paper.

5 Place a cover, the spacer, and a hinge piece, with their sides touching, on the pasted bookcloth. Quickly adjust them so there is an even margin of bookcloth extending around each side.

Remove the spacer, then cut triangles from each corner of the bookcloth, leaving an extension equal to two thicknesses of the book-board, so you can cover the corners well.

6   With the bone folder, pull the head side of the bookcloth margin up and over the edge of the bookboard and rub down well. With the point of the bone folder, push down the tiny piece of bookcloth you will see extending at each corner. Rub the bone folder into the crevice between the cover and hinge to be sure the bookcloth adheres there.

Repeat this procedure at the tail, then the spine, then fore edge sides of the cover. Turn the cover over and rub the bone folder over the surface to flatten out any air bubbles. Gently rock the flat of the bone folder over each pointy corner to soften it.

Repeat with the other cover.

7   Measure and cut lining paper so it reaches to within ¼ inch from each edge of the cover.

Paste it in the same way you pasted the bookcloth in step 4. Then flip the lining paper over onto the uncovered side of the bookboard; smooth out any air bubbles and rub to adhere.

Wrap both covers in scrap paper and let them sit under a weight until dry — at least 4 hours, or overnight.

8   Meanwhile, make the text block. To measure, cut, fold, and make holes in the text pages, follow steps 1 through 3 under "How to Make a Softcover Album" on pages 82 – 85, except make three evenly spaced holes in the text pages with an awl. Set aside the text pages until you are ready to assemble the album.

9   Hold the text pages together and tap them on the spine side to be sure they're aligned; clamp them together, leaving the spine side free.

10 With an awl, make three holes in the cover hinge pieces that align with the holes in the text block.

11 Assemble the album by flattening the back cover and laying it on a clean work surface, with the hinge to your left and the cover's fore edge to your right. (The side covered with bookcloth will be facing you.)

Put the clamped text block down so just the folded edge of the text block is on top of the hinge piece of the cover and the holes in the cover and text are aligned. (The fore edge side of the text block will be to your left.)

Flatten the front cover and lay it down with its lined side facing you (its side covered with bookcloth facing down) and its holes directly over the holes in the text. (The covers will be facing each other with their right sides together.)

12 With the text pages still clamped together, sew the covers and text block together with linen thread and a needle in a figure eight, and tie securely with a square knot. Remove the clamps.

To Make a Portfolio

Materials you need for making a portfolio:

bookboard

pencil

straightedge

craft knife or paper cutter

bookcloth to match or
    contrast cover paper

scrap paper

mixture of 50/50 PVA/starch
    paste adhesive

paste brush

bone folder

100% PVA adhesive

decorative cover paper that
    is strong but flexible

ribbon or cotton twill for ties

decorative paper to line
    boards

weight

1   Check the bookboard's grain and draw a pencil line along it.

Determine the portfolio's size, then cut two sheets of bookboard to that size with a straightedge and craft knife or a paper cutter, with the grain running parallel to the spine side.

Decide how much of the portfolio cover will be covered with bookcloth, then draw a line on each of the bookboards to use later as a guideline for placing the bookcloth.

2   Measure and cut two pieces of bookcloth with the grain running the same way as the bookboard's grain: measure the first piece as long as the height of the book plus $3/4$-inch extensions on the head and tail ends. This piece should be wide enough to reach around the spine side of the bookboards from one guideline to the other plus a margin equal to three thicknesses of the bookboard. Two pieces of cut bookcloth are shown in the photograph of materials.

For example, if the height of your portfolio is 12 inches and you have determined that the bookcloth will cover 3 inches of each cover, and the bookboard is $1/4$ inch thick, your bookcloth should be $6\,3/4$ inches wide (3 inches on each side plus 3 times the board's thickness) and $13\,1/2$ inches long (the height of the portfolio plus $3/4$ inch on each end).

Measure another piece of bookcloth the exact length as the height of the portfolio — with no extension allowance — and the same width as the first piece of bookcloth.

3   Place the first (the longer) piece of bookcloth face down on a sheet of scrap paper. Brush the back of the bookcloth with mixture of 50/50 PVA/starch paste, beginning each stroke in the middle and pulling out beyond the edges. Discard the scrap paper.

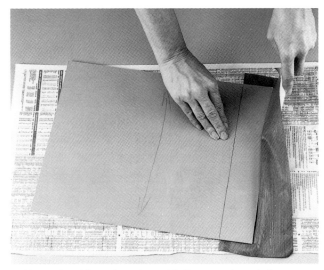

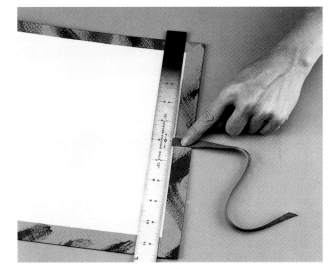

4 Turn a bookboard so the guideline you drew is face up. With the pasted side of the bookcloth up, lay the bookboard on the pasted bookcloth so that the long edge of the bookcloth meets the guideline. Repeat the procedure with the other bookboard, adding a little more paste if it has dried.

Now you have both bookboards adhered to one piece of bookcloth, with a margin between them that allows space for placing papers in the portfolio. Rub the bookcloth well on both sides with the flat side of a bone folder to be sure the bookcloth adheres.

5 Brush a little more paste mixture onto the bookcloth extensions, then fold them over the head and tail of the bookboards; with the point of the bone folder, vigorously rub the extensions into the groove between the bookboards.

6 Cut the cover paper and cover the boards in the same manner described on pages 73 – 74, steps 23 through 30.

7 After the boards are covered, apply the closure ties. Cut two lengths of ribbon or twill tape about 12 inches long. Open the portfolio; measure and lightly mark positions where you want the ties on the fore edge sides of the portfolio covers. Apply 100% PVA to 1 inch of one end of each ribbon and attach them at the marks.

(The lining paper will cover the glued-down ends of the ties and the edges of the inside bookcloth.)

Note: At this point, you can attach more than two ribbons if you like. Consider attaching closure ties at the head, tail, *and* fore edge sides. Or if your portfolio is large, attach two or three closure ties at the fore edge.

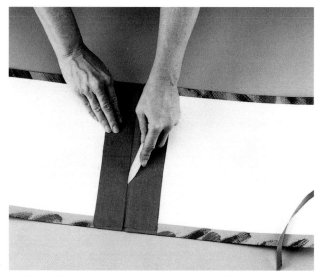

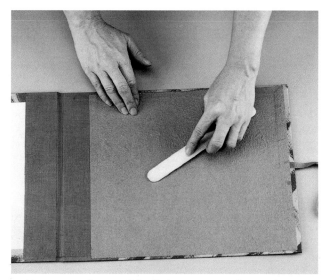

8 Place the second — shorter — piece of bookcloth on scrap paper and brush it with mixture of 50/50 PVA/starch paste, then open the portfolio and carefully lay the strip of bookcloth centered on the inside spine of the portfolio, matching the ends at the head and tail. (Now you have a double thickness of bookcloth to support the spine.) Rub the bookcloth down thoroughly into the grooves with the edge of the bone folder.

9 Measure 2 sheets of the lining paper so that each covers the inside of a board to within ¼ inch of the head, tail, and fore edge sides and covers ¼ inch of the edge of the inside bookcloth. Be sure the grain of the lining paper matches the grain of the board and the cover paper.

Place one sheet of the paper face down on scrap paper and brush it thoroughly with mixture of 50/50 PVA/starch paste. Begin every stroke in the center and pull the brush out beyond the edge of the paper. Open the portfolio and carefully place the lining paper on one bookboard, adjusting so the paper is within ¼ inch of each edge. Repeat with the other sheet of lining paper. Smooth the lining with your fingers or bone folder to make sure it adheres.

10 Place several layers of scrap paper inside and outside the portfolio and let it dry under a weight for at least 4 hours, or overnight.

The finished portfolio is covered with pastel paper painted with zigzags of acrylic paint.

Chapter Eight

Multisignature Hardcover Books

For people who love books, making, holding, and using a handmade hardcover book may be the ultimate creative reward. By making your own book, you can choose its size, thickness, and colors (inside and out) and then use it in any way you like.

Book artists choose a theme and plan the layout of a new book, often sketching out every page, then printing, writing, or drawing on the pages before they're bound. Or they make blank books — sometimes in classic proportions and sometimes longer or wider than expected — for keeping thoughts, poems, or drawings.

Many book lovers find that a handmade book they can use — to record their dreams, thoughts, and growth, to spew disappointment or anger, to make a political statement, or to propose solutions to human dilemmas — becomes a precious talisman. And many fortunate families have treasured personal journals kept by their forebears as they met their own challenges in other decades and centuries.

Regardless of the use, size, or colors employed, making a multisignature hardcover book is a long and involved process. Be sure to use the highest-quality papers and boards you can find and afford,

because you'll want to know that the book you've spent time making will survive a very long time; it may become an heirloom for your own descendants.

Art supply stores and catalogs offer beautiful papers — marbled, paste paint, printed, textured, block printed, handmade with or without flecks of flowers or glitter — in a fabulous array of colors. As long as the paper is thin enough to be flexible, it can be used to cover the book you make. Remember, too, that you can decorate your own cover paper with paste paint or potato prints or pen-and-ink drawings. And bookcloth can be a subdued color or a printed fabric that you've made yourself, as described in Chapter Two.

Classic endpapers are marbled, but any lightweight strong paper will serve. Again, you can decorate it yourself if you like. Or consider having a favorite photograph color-copied — with the size blown up, if needed — to make endpapers. Text paper can be textured or smooth, preferably of bond weight.

Sewing several signatures together requires sewing in tapes to stabilize the spine and a "kettle" stitch, which helps secure the sections together at the head and tail. We don't know the etymology of the word "kettle," but it probably

The signatures in a handmade book
are easily discernible.

derives from a German or Dutch word. Take your time while sewing the signatures and enjoy the repetition; it gets easier with every section you sew.

Bookbinding is an art and skill that has its own set of equipment — some of it heavy and expensive. But in this chapter, you'll learn how to make a hardcover book with a minimum number of tools.

While the techniques may be a little different than those you would use in a bookbinding studio, you'll be pleased with the results of your work. The first part of making your book involves folding and sewing the signatures together, and the second part is casing in the text, which is much like making a hardcover single-signature book, as described in Chapter Six.

The cover paper for a handwritten cookbook was printed with a linoleum cut and ink before it was pasted onto the bookboard.

Bookbinding is
an honored craft
in Florence, Italy,
where these books
were made.

To Sew Signatures Together

Materials you need for sewing signatures together:

text paper (preferably bond weight)

paper cutter, craft knife, or rotary cutter

bone folder

scrap paper

ruler

pencil

linen or cotton twill tape, $\frac{1}{2}$, $\frac{3}{8}$, or $\frac{5}{8}$ inches wide

awl or large darning needle (for punching holes)

strong thread (linen, cotton, or silk)

darning needle

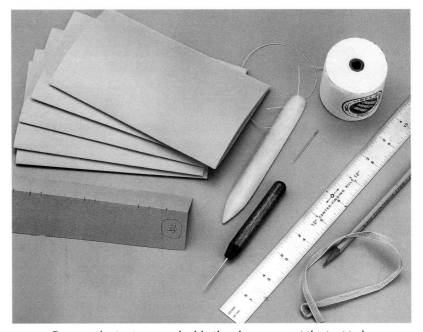

1 Prepare the text paper: decide the size you want the text to be, then cut the text paper to the height and twice the width of the finished size. For example, if the finished size will be 10 inches high and 8 inches wide, cut your text paper 10 by 16 inches. (Each signature usually consists of 5 to 8 sheets, but the number of signatures you make is unlimited.)

2 Fold each sheet, one at a time, and rub the crease with a bone folder. As you fold the sheets, arrange them in stacks of 5 to 8 sheets each — these stacks become signatures. Stack the signatures with the spine and fore edges alternating and place them under a heavy weight for 24 hours to flatten them.

3 Cut a piece of scrap paper exactly the same height as the text paper and 3 inches wide to be used as a hole-punch guide. Fold the scrap paper in half lengthwise and write "top" in any corner, to indicate the head end of the book.

The zing of exciting
color can be on the
outside or inside the
covers of your
handmade books.

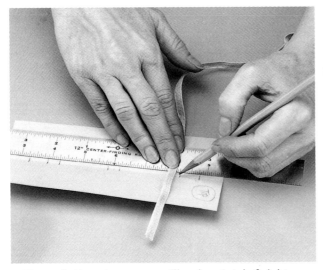

4 To sew in three tapes, you will make a total of eight holes. Measure and mark the holes on the scrap paper. First, unfold the scrap paper and, in the fold, make dark pencil marks ½ inch from the head (marked "top") and tail ends. With a ruler, find the middle of the paper and make a light mark there. Center a piece of linen tape on the middle mark and make darker marks at each side of the tape. Erase the light pencil mark.

5 In the same way, make two more tape-wide marks equidistant from the middle of the paper and the mark ½ inch from the head and again ½ inch from the tail. You now have eight dark marks.

6 Place the guide sheet face up inside a folded signature and make holes with the awl through all thicknesses at the eight dark marks on the guide paper. Paying attention to which corner is the "top" of each signature, carefully stack the punched signatures so that the top of each one is in the same position.

7 Cut a length of thread no more than five times the height of the book. Any more thread will get tangled. (If you run out of thread, attach another length of thread with a small weaver's knot: make a slip knot in the end of the new thread in a place inside the fold of a signature, put the end of the old thread in the slip knot, and pull the slip knot tight until it "clicks" into place and holds the new thread.)

8 Now cut three lengths of linen tape, each long enough to cover the depth of the spine plus about 1 ½ inches to overhang on each side of the text block. Put the pieces of tape loosely in place on the spine of the first signature.

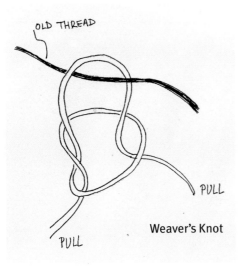

OLD THREAD

PULL

PULL

Weaver's Knot

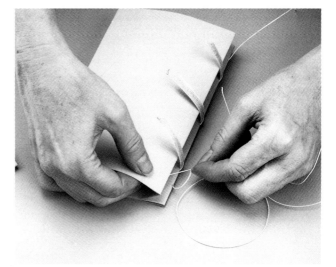

9 With one strand of thread in the needle, begin sewing by pushing the needle through the first hole at the head, from the outside into the fold of the first signature. Leave a 3-inch tail of thread hanging outside of the signature.

10 The needle is now on the inside. Push it through the next hole, from the inside to the outside. Then take the needle and thread over the tape and push the needle to the inside through the third hole, thereby securing the first piece of tape. The needle never pierces the linen tapes. The tension of the thread should be firm, but not tight.

11 The needle is again on the inside. Repeat the previous step, taking the needle through each successive hole, until all three tapes are secure and you have pulled the needle to the outside through the last (eighth) hole at the tail.

12 Place the second signature on the first (be sure the "top" corner of the second signature matches the "top" of the first). Push the needle through the adjacent hole at the tail, from the outside to inside. Repeat the in-and-out sewing, continuing to secure the tapes under the thread, until you're again at the head of the book and the needle is on the outside of the second signature.

Attach the third signature in the same way.

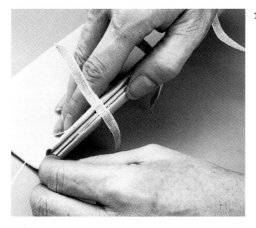

13 Now make the first kettle stitch, which secures the first and second sections. Take a close look at the thread that joins the first and second signatures, which runs perpendicular to the spine. Slip the needle under that thread and gently pull the thread until there is a small loop. Pull the needle through that loop and gently tug the thread to firm the stitch, but don't pull it very tight. (See the kettle stitch diagram, right, for further guidance.)

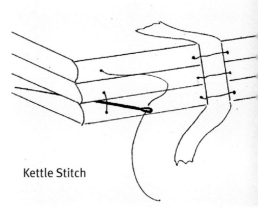

Kettle Stitch

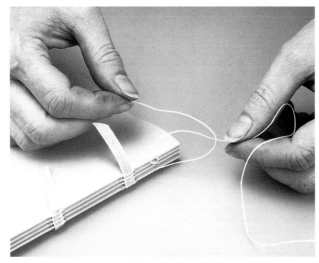

14 Refer to step 12 and sew the fourth signature onto the third signature in the same way.

15 At this point, your needle is on the outside of the fourth signature adjacent to the 3-inch tail of thread you left hanging at the beginning of the sewing process (step 10). With a square knot, tie the thread still in the needle to the loose 3-inch tail of thread, but don't cut the thread from the needle.

16 Continue to add signatures in the same way, making a kettle stitch between the signatures every time you bring the needle out of the last hole at both the head *and* tail ends.

17 After all the signatures are sewn together, secure the thread before cutting it from the needle: make two or three kettle stitches — one below the other under the other kettle stitches of the last two or three signatures you've sewn in — then cut off both ends of the thread, leaving tail ends of about ½ inch.

Your multisignature text block is now securely joined, and the tapes are in place but still loose — be very careful that the tapes don't get pulled out.

18 Turn the ends of the tapes so they are lying on and under the text block; then place heavy weights on top for 24 hours to flatten the tapes, or lightly pound the spine with a hammer before casing in.

The process
of making
hardcover
multisignature
books is long,
but very
rewarding.

To Case in a Multisignature Hardcover Book

Materials you need for casing in a multisignature hardcover book:

sewn text block (see "To Sew Signatures Together" on page 98)

100% PVA adhesive

glue brush

light weight (such as a book)

craft knife, paper cutter, or rotary cutter

endpaper (marbled paper, quality gift wrap, or decorated bond paper)

scrap paper

bone folder

bookcloth — any color — for hinge

kraft paper

scissors or craft knife

household sponge

small piece of bookcloth for headband (optional)

string for headband (optional)

bookboard

pencil

bookcloth to match or contrast cover paper for spine

mixture of 50/50 PVA/starch paste

$\frac{1}{4}$-inch acrylic spacer, or a spacer cut from bookboard exactly $\frac{1}{4}$ inch wide and at least 6 inches long

straightedge

decorative cover paper that is strong but flexible

plastic wrap or Mylar® heavy weight

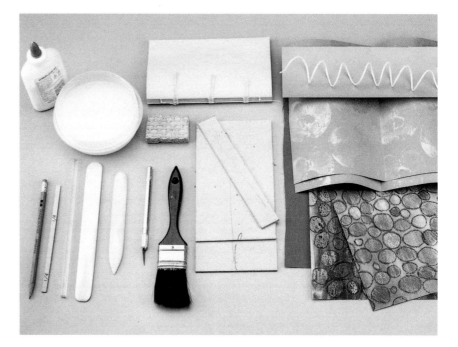

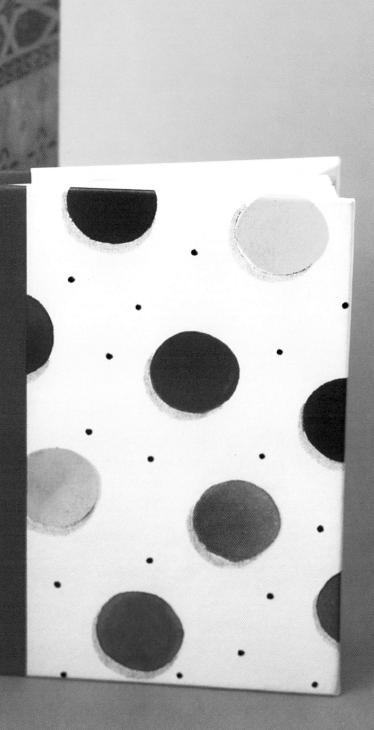

Multisignature hardcover books covered with best-quality gift wrap paper and bookcloth.

1 Hold the text block firmly in one hand and with a brush apply 100% PVA to only the spine, tapping the bristles of the brush between the signatures and onto the tapes. Be sure the ends of the tapes are lying flat on the front and back of the text block. Place the text block under a light weight for 30 minutes to dry.

2 Meanwhile, cut two sheets of endpaper the same size as the text paper *before* it was folded into signatures. (In the example on page 98, the text paper for a 10-by-8-inch text block was cut 10 by 16 inches.)

3 Apply the endpaper: with scrap paper, mask the text block, leaving about $\frac{1}{4}$ inch of the text block exposed at the spine side; brush a thin layer of 100% PVA onto the exposed portion of the text block and the tapes.

4 Fold the endpaper with the design to the *inside,* so the undecorated side of the endpaper is outside. Align all sides of the endpaper and the text block. Use a bone folder to rub the endpaper onto the glued edge of the book. But, unlike the photo at left, *be sure the ends of the tapes are on the outside of the endpapers.*

Repeat on the other side of the text block with the other endpaper.

5 To make the hinge (which will be completely hidden when the book is finished), cut a piece of bookcloth (any color) the same height as the text block and wide enough to wrap around the spine with $1\frac{1}{2}$ inches extending on both sides. Trim triangles off all four corners — a step not shown in the photograph.

6 Brush 100% PVA onto only the spine of the book and rub well the bookcloth hinge onto the spine. (The hinge will be attached at the spine only.)

7 Cut a strip of kraft paper exactly the same size as the spine — with no extensions on any side. Place it on a sheet of scrap paper and brush it with 100% PVA, then, with a damp sponge, rub the glued side of the kraft paper onto the spine. Set aside to dry. This additional layer of paper helps stabilize and strengthen the spine.

8 A decorative headband is optional but a nice finishing element for a book. If you're not applying a headband, skip to step 11.

With the same or contrasting bookcloth you've used to cover the spine, cut a rectangle about 1 inch wide and twice as long as the spine is wide plus 1 inch extra.

Cut a piece of string 1 inch longer than this piece of bookcloth is wide.

Brush the "wrong" side of the bookcloth with 100% PVA; pull the string taut and place it along the center of the bookcloth. Fold the bookcloth over the string. Rub the bone folder along the edge of the string on one side only to make an indentation.

9 Hold the headband against the spine to measure, then cut it so it is exactly as long as the spine is wide. Make two — one for the head and one for the tail of the book. The side of the headband that is *indented* goes against the head and tail of the spine.

10 Brush one side of the headband with 100% PVA, then affix the headband to the head of the spine of the text block so that the bump the string makes extends slightly beyond the edge of the spine. Repeat on the tail end of the text block.

11 Cut three pieces of bookboard — two covers and a spine board.

   Measure then cut the bookboard for the back and front covers: each cover measures *1/8 inch larger* on the head, tail, and fore edge sides than the text block; the spine side of the covers measures *1/4 inch less* than the width of the text block.

12 To measure how wide to cut the spine board, sandwich the text block between the two covers and hold them together in one hand. Wrap a narrow strip of scrap paper around the "sandwich," then make pencil marks on the scrap paper at the outside edges on the spine side of the front and back covers.

   Cut the spine board the same height as the covers and the same width as the paper strip measurement.

13 Decide how far you want the bookcloth on the spine to extend onto the covers of the book. For example, if you want the bookcloth to extend 2 inches onto the covers, measure 2 inches from the spine edge of the book-boards and draw lines as placement guides. Measure then cut the bookcloth 3/4 inch longer on both ends than the height of the book. The width of the bookcloth should be wide enough to cover the spine plus enough to extend onto the covers to your specifications.

14 Place the bookcloth you just cut on a sheet of scrap paper, face down, and brush the back with mixture of 50/50 PVA/starch paste, beginning every stroke in the middle and pulling the brush out just beyond the edges of the bookcloth.

 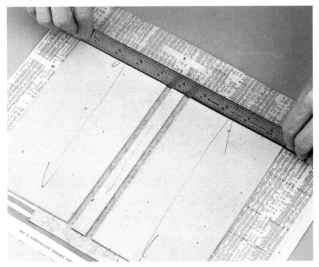

15 Quickly arrange a cover, a spacer, and the spine board on the bookcloth with a ³/₄-inch overhang on each end.

16 Move the spacer to the other side of the spine piece and align the other cover onto the bookcloth, using a straightedge to be sure the covers and spine pieces are all exactly aligned. (The spaces between the covers and spine are necessary to open the book.)

17 With the bone folder, pull the overhanging ends of the bookcloth onto the inside of the covers and spine. If the paste has dried, apply a little more. Vigorously rub the bone folder into the grooves between the spine board and the covers until the grooves stay put.

18 Measure and cut two sheets of cover paper, each to extend ³/₄ inch beyond the head, tail, and fore edge of the covers; the spine side should extend to just slightly cover the edge of the bookcloth by about ¹/₈ inch.

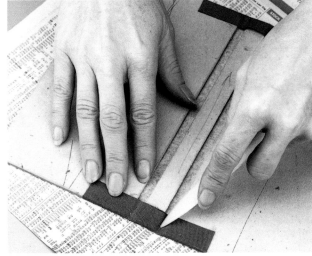

19 Turn the cover paper face down on scrap paper, then brush the back with mixture of 50/50 PVA/starch paste.

20 Carefully place the pasted paper just over the edge of the bookcloth, making sure that the edges extend evenly (3/4 inch) at the head, tail, and fore edge. You have a little time to make adjustments before the paste dries.

21 With a craft knife or scissors, cut triangles off the corners at the head and tail ends of the fore edge side, leaving a margin of paper at each corner equal to twice the thickness of the bookboard, which allows you to cover the board's corners securely with paper.

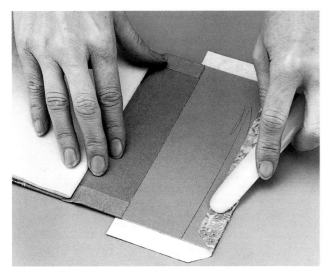

22 With the flat side of the bone folder, raise the fore edge of the paper up and over the bookboard and rub it well on the top and edge. Use the point of the bone folder to rub down the tiny edge of the paper extending at each corner, which helps cover the corner smoothly.

23 Raise and fold the head side of the paper over the bookboard and rub it well on the top and the edge.

24 Raise and fold over the tail side.

25 Roll the flat of the bone folder gently over the corners to flatten any points that have formed. Then rub the outside of the book with your fingers or the flat side of the bone folder to smooth out any air bubbles.

26 The case is made. Now you case in the text block.

27 First you attach the linen tapes on the text block to the case. Cover the free ends of the linen tapes with a small amount of 100% PVA, then open the case flat on the work surface and place the spine of the text block directly on the spine of the case. Stick the tapes onto the endpapers of the text block and smooth the tapes down well with your fingers.

28 Now paste the hinges onto the cover. (The tapes and the hinge act together to hold the text block firmly in the case.)

Open one cover of the case. To prevent paste from getting on the endpapers, mask one endpaper with scrap paper, leaving the hinge exposed, and brush the hinge with as little mixture of 50/50 PVA/starch paste as possible, so the paste won't ooze out when the hinge is smoothed down.

29 With the bone folder, thoroughly rub the hinge down onto the inside cover. Carefully wipe away any paste that might escape from the edges. Repeat these last two steps on the other side of the case.

30 Prepare to paste down the endpapers: with the book closed, place it flat on the work surface; open one cover and place a sheet of scrap paper between the endpaper and the first page of text to protect the text from paste. Brush 100% starch paste onto the undecorated side of the endpaper. Begin each brush stroke at the center of the paper and pull the brush out to just beyond the edges. Remove the scrap paper.

31 Leave the cover that is being attached flat on the work surface. Slowly and carefully bring the other cover and text block up and over so the pasted endpaper eases onto the bookboard; rub the closed cover with your hand or the bone folder to smooth the endpaper, but do not open the book. Turn the book to its other side and repeat these last two steps with the other cover.

32 While the paste is still damp, rub the bone folder well into the grooves between the spine and the covers. If you like, protect the bookcloth with scrap paper to prevent marking the bookcloth.

33 To be sure the groove is well established as the case dries, wrap a piece of string around the book, with the string resting in the groove, and tighten it by rotating a pencil at one end.

34 Without opening the book, slip plastic wrap or Mylar® between the cover and the text so that the damp of the cover doesn't filter into the text block. (The reason you shouldn't open the cover is that doing so would pull the endpaper out of alignment.) Place several layers of scrap paper beneath and on top of the book to absorb extra moisture. Place a heavy weight on the book until dry, changing scrap paper as it gets damp. Depending on the climate, drying time is at least 8 hours and can be up to 24 hours.

Chapter Nine

Designing Your Handmade Books

ou can get inspiration for color, design, and content for your handmade books from a bowl of fruit, a favorite painting, kitchen wallpaper, a landscape, the pattern on a quilt or carpet, a postcard, a potted plant, children's drawings, stacks of firewood, dolls in a gift shop — in other words, just about anywhere. Or you may have a theme in mind, such as birth, a holiday, the solar system, friendship, food and cooking, your family, a favorite place or city, machines, hearts, flowers, or animals.

Once you've chosen a design or theme, you can decide how you want to convey your ideas. Go to an art supply store that has a large selection of paper or search art catalogs for papers you can buy through mail order. You might also take a look in shops that carry gift wrap or other decorated papers to see if there are preprinted papers that fit your idea.

Remember, too, that you can individualize books with bookcloth made with printed fabric (see "To Make Bookcloth," page 24) to cover part or all of the cover of a book. Look at the array of printed cottons in fabric stores — you can find prints that depict just about any theme, from international flags to cooking to teddy bears to golf and football.

You may express your design on only the front cover or throughout the book, from cover to cover.

For example, if you want a garden design and decide to make a single-signature book, you can simply paste a photograph of a garden on the front cover or make the cover with a flower-print paper.

Take the same example a step further: your garden theme is how your garden changes throughout the year, and the format you choose is an accordion book. You can make book covers with drawings or printed paper of herbs or flowers. Perhaps you'd like to take pictures of your garden several times during the year to chronicle its changes and put the photos and handwritten captions in your book — accordions make ideal photo albums because they expand so nicely. Or if you like to draw or paint, make the book with drawing paper (90-pound) or watercolor paper (140-pound) and use it as a sketchbook.

When you get home from a vacation and sort through your photographs and postcards, consider making a special album. Play with the photographs by cropping some yourself with scissors or have them professionally enlarged or reduced. Take photos to be copied. Color copy machines can change color photos into sepia tones or shades of gray, pink, yellow — whatever you like. Your album can be as simple as mounting the photographs on bristol board or heavy paper, then making a hole in one or two corners of each mounting board and

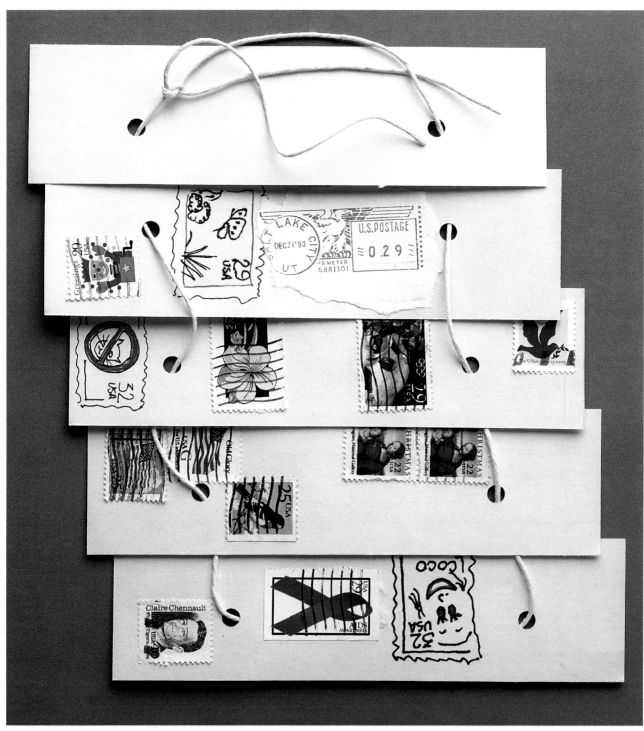

Pacific Rim leaf books inspired this book that is decorated with stamps and drawings of stamps.

attaching them with a ring or tying them loosely together with ribbon.

You don't have to know how to draw to make books or design your own cover and lining materials. Experiment with block printing, for example. Dip a sponge, car keys, a cork, a fork, or the edge of corrugated cardboard into water-soluble or oil-based paint, then print it onto paper in random or planned designs. Or spray water onto a sheet of paper, then drop water-soluble paint onto it to see what happens.

You can create new designs by drawing abstract shapes on paper with crayons, then painting over the entire sheet with tempera or watercolor paint. The waxy crayon resists the paint, but the background absorbs the new color, and you'll be surprised at the variety of effects you can get.

Sometimes you may see a design, drawing, or photograph that you would like to incorporate into a book but don't think you can copy it freehand. Perhaps as you've looked at pictures in this book or recall other handmade books you've seen, you have been inspired to make something similar. One easy way to transfer designs is with carbon paper:

Supplies you need for transferring designs with carbon paper:

original design

paper on which to make the transfer

carbon paper

masking tape

pen or pencil

pastels or other coloring agents, such as paints or colored pencils

To Transfer Designs

1 In this case, the original design was enlarged with a copy machine.

2 Place on the work surface the paper you want the design to go onto and cover it with the carbon paper, carbon side down, and tape just the corners to secure the paper and carbon paper.

3 Place the design you want to copy face up over the carbon paper in the position that puts the design in the place you like on the paper you're copying onto. With a pen or pencil, outline the design, pressing hard enough to make an impression from the carbon paper onto the paper.

You can easily see where you have traced by the lines your pen leaves on the design. With some designs, you want to transfer every detail, while others may require only an abstract outline.

4 Remove the original design and carbon paper to reveal the transferred design.

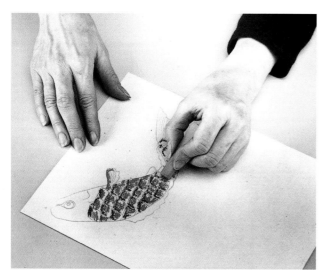

5 Color or paint the design.

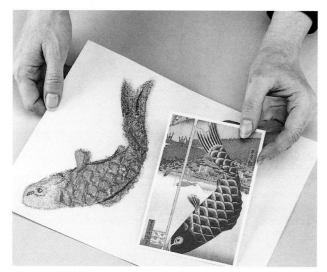

6 Now you have the essence — if not an exact
   duplicate — of the original design.

**The design
was completed
by placing
coins under
the paper, then
rubbing
crayons over
them to make
"bubbles."**

Lacquer transfers from photocopies can make fascinating images.

Transferring an Image with Lacquer Thinner

Another transfer technique is useful when the paper you are using for your book project is too thick or too large to go through a copy machine. It will make a mirror image of the design you want to copy, which is important to remember because any type will transfer backwards.

You must work in a well-ventilated area and follow all the precautions on the can of lacquer thinner.

First, make a copy of your design on a black-and-white or color copier. Brush lacquer thinner onto the front surface of the copy, then very quickly place the wet side down on the paper that will receive the image, and rub the back of the wet paper briskly and thoroughly with a baren (a rubbing device used in printmaking) or the back of a wooden spoon.

The lacquer thinner will partially dissolve the copier's ink, but you have to work fast because it dries quickly.

Check the transfer by carefully pulling the top paper away. Repeat with more lacquer thinner if you need to, being careful to replace the image in the same place.

Crayons
resist water-
soluble
paint and
can be used
to make
abstract
designs
for covering
books.

Glossary

accordion
a book made by folding a long sheet of paper back and forth; covers can be soft or hard

awl
sometimes called a "potter's tool" by bookbinders, a wood-handled awl makes holes for binding

bond paper
very common paper used in printers and copy machines, available from office suppliers in many colors but limited sizes; a good choice for text paper in single- and multisignature handmade books

bone folder
a flat tool made of bone, often with one end pointed and the other rounded, used extensively in bookbinding for folding, molding, scoring, lifting damp edges, etc. Care for it by soaking in vegetable oil for 24 hours once or twice a year, then washing well with soap and warm water. Wooden tongue depressors are acceptable substitutes

bookboard
pressed acid-free cardboard, sometimes called binder's board or millboard, available from bookbinding suppliers in various weights, usually about $\frac{1}{32}$ inch to $\frac{1}{8}$ inch thick; heavy bristol board is a good substitute; for large portfolios, thin particleboard or plywood can be used in the same way

bookcloth
fabric that has been adhered to strong, lightweight paper with paste, which prevents the fabric's stretch and prevents paste from soaking through the fabric

brass fasteners
clasps used to hold papers together; a simple device made with two prongs that are spread apart after the fastener is inserted through a hole

card stock
thin, stiff cardboard, such as file folders are made from

case
a hardback cover for a book before the text block is attached

case in
to attach a text block to a case

Chicago screws
two-piece screws — one "male" and the other "female"; the female side has a smooth outside shank, and both have flat tops; available at hardware stores

codex (codices)
books made of folded and sewn signatures

craft knife
a knife with a replaceable blade, such as a #11 X-Acto; for cutting heavy boards, a carpet knife or box cutter is optional

crossgrain
opposite the grainline; paper and bookboard will not tear or fold evenly or smoothly on the crossgrain

cutting mat
"self-healing" mats protect work surfaces and come in many sizes; the mat should be hard rather than spongy; available at fabric and art supply stores

drill
a hand-cranked or electric drill goes through a thick stack of paper or boards, but tends to grind rather than make a smooth hole; for most bookbinding applications, an awl is preferable

endpapers
folded sheets of paper, often decorated, that are attached on both sides of a text block to form a lining and (flyleaf) for the inside covers of a book

flyleaf
paper, usually decorative, that lines a book's covers and lies loosely on the text block

fore edge
the side of the book opposite the spine

grainline
the direction that fibers run in machine-made paper and bookboard; the grain is formed during papermaking when pulp fibers align in parallel formation

head
the top of the book

height
the measurement from the head to the tail of a book

Japanese or washi papers
often erroneously called "rice paper," these strong, lightweight papers are made from long-fibered kozo, gampi, and mitsumata plants with little or no chemical additives; most often listed and sold as washi, the papers are available in many colors, various textures and weights; and some are stenciled or stamped with designs. They can be purchased from well-stocked art supply stores or by mail order and used for making Japanese-bound books, as well as scrolls and hard- or softcover books.

kettle stitch
a stitch used when sewing several signatures together, which secures the sections at head and tail; "kettle" is probably a derivative of a German or Dutch word

linen twill tape
finely woven fabric tape available from bookbinding suppliers in $3/8$-, $1/2$-, or $5/8$-inch widths; fine cotton twill tape, available from dressmaking supply shops, is an acceptable substitute but do not use polyester or rayon tape

methyl cellulose
a natural dry substance that when mixed with water makes an adhesive; wallpaper paste is an example

mixture
a mixture of glue and starch paste, usually 50/50, used for adhering paper to bookboards and other tasks; the glue strengthens the adhesion and the paste slows the drying time

paper scissors
scissors with very long blades or any scissors that can stand up to the rigors of cutting paper

papyrus
the forerunner of paper, made from reeds that have been flattened and pressed together to form paperlike sheets

pastel paper
heavy paper with a rough texture that is made especially for drawing with pastels, but is of good weight for some handmade book applications

PVA (polyvinyl acetate)
a quick-drying white glue that dries clear and stays flexible; any white glue is a good substitute

"rice paper"
see Japanese papers

rotary cutter
a plastic handle holds a very sharp circular blade that cuts as it's rolled across paper, fabric, or film; available from quilting suppliers

score
to indent a line in the fibers of paper along the grainline so it can be folded easily; usually done with the sharp edge of a bone folder run along a straightedge

scroll
a style of book made of a long sheet of paper that is attached and rolled onto one or two rods

signature
a stack of sheets of paper folded in the center then sewn or stapled together; also called a section or a folio

sliding report holders
clasps that easily adjust to accommodate various thicknesses of stacks of single sheets of paper; often used to bind legal documents; available at office supply stores

spacer
a narrow strip of premeasured and cut bookboard placed between two objects (usually the cover and hinge pieces of a hard cover) used to ensure that the space between the two is exactly even; 1/4-inch spacers made of acrylic are available from quilting suppliers and are ideal for bookbinding applications

spine
the side of a book where the signatures or single sheets are attached

spring divider
a tool that aids in making accurately spaced divisions and other measuring jobs; available from drafting suppliers and art supply stores

square
the margin of cover that extends beyond the book's text block, usually ⅛ inch

starch paste
a simple and very effective adhesive for many bookbinding projects; a mixture of cornstarch or rice flour mixed with boiling water; paste is water soluble when dry and removable, so is archival (recipe on pages 26 – 27)

straightedge
a metal straightedge — not plastic — for guiding long cuts with a craft knife

T square
metal and at least 12 inches long or a metal triangle with right angles, used to check square corners

tail
the bottom of the book, opposite the head

text or text block
the pages of the book whether folded in an accordion, joined into signatures, or as bound single sheets

thread
linen thread, which comes in various weights from bookbinding suppliers and catalogs, is best for book-binding, but 100 percent cotton or silk is a good substitute; do not use polyester or cotton-covered polyester

washi papers
see Japanese papers

width
a book's measurement from the spine to the fore edge

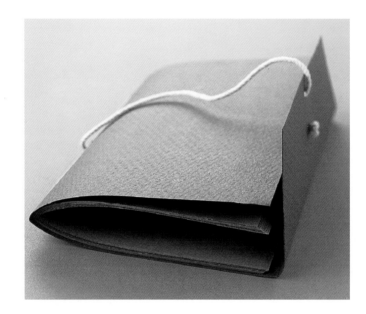